Lonely 🌐 planet

POCKET

LONDON

TOP EXPERIENCES • LOCAL LIFE

T0018115

EMILIE FILOU, TASMIN WABY

Contents

Plan Your Trip 4

Elizabeth Tower & Big Ben (p57)
THÜRLER BAPTISTE/SHUTTERSTOCK ©

Welcome to London

London has something for everyone, from grand museums, dazzling architecture and opulent royalty to striking diversity, glorious parks and irrepressible pizzazz. It's immersed in history, but London is also a tireless innovator of culture and creative talent. A cosmopolitan dynamism makes it one of the world's most international cities, yet one that remains somehow intrinsically British.

London's Top Experiences

Wander through time at the British Museum (p90)

Stand in awe of St Paul's Cathedral (p108)

Get with the trends at Tate Modern (p130)

Explore nature at the Natural History Museum (p152)

See the Crown Jewels at the Tower of London (p112)

Visit Kings and Queens at Westminster Abbey (p50)

Walk the stately Houses of Parliament (p56)

Review European art history at the National Gallery (p70)

Stroll among artworks at Victoria & Albert Museum (p148)

Tour regal Hampton Court Palace (p200)

Wave at royalty at Buckingham Palace (p54)

See stars at the Royal Observatory & Greenwich Park (p194)

Dining Out

London's dining scene is up there with the world's best, though it pays to do your research: there's plenty of mediocre options here. The city's strongest asset is its incredible diversity: from street-food markets to high-end dining (with epic views) – and global cuisines from Afghan to Zambian – it's an A to Z of foodie experiences.

World Food

One of the joys of eating out in London is the sheer choice. For historical reasons, Indian cuisine is widely available, and Asian cuisines in general are popular. You'll find dozens of Chinese, Thai, Vietnamese Japanese and Korean restaurants, as well as elaborate fusion establishments blending flavours from different parts of Asia.

Middle Eastern cuisine is also well covered. Continental European cuisines – French, Italian, Spanish, Greek, Scandinavian etc – are easy to find, with many excellent modern European establishments. Sometimes you'll find restaurants serving similar cuisines congregating in neighbourhoods where their community is based.

British Food

Modern British food has become a cuisine in its own right, championing traditional ingredients such as root vegetables, smoked fish, shellfish, game, salt-marsh lamb, sausages, black pudding, offal, secondary cuts of meat and bone marrow.

Gastropubs

Traditionally pubs in London were where you went for a drink, with maybe a packet of potato crisps to soak up the alcohol. Since the birth of the gastropub in the 1990s, just about every establishment serves full meals. The quality varies widely, from microwaved dishes to vegan choices and Michelin-starred cuisine with impressive wine lists.

BHARAT RAWAIL/SHUTTERSTOCK ©

Best British

St. JOHN The restaurant that inspired the revival of British cuisine. (p121)

Dinner by Heston Blumenthal Winning celebration of British cuisine, with both traditional and modern accents. (p163)

Launceston Place Magnificent food, presentation and service. (p163)

Foyer & Reading Room at Claridge's Afternoon tea in aristocratic style. (p81)

Best European

Padella Cheap and flavourful homemade pasta in Borough Market. (pictured above; p139)

Skylon Stunning Thames vistas; fine international menu. (p141)

Delaunay Grand mittel-European ambience and menu. (p83)

Spring Sumptuous venue with an organic seasonal menu. (p80)

Best of the Rest

Smoking Goat Exceptional Thai in mod-industrial surrounds. (p190)

Kanada-Ya Join the queue for its superb *tonkotsu* ramen. (p82)

Honey & Co Exquisite Middle Eastern in a pocket-sized Bloomsbury dining room. (p100)

Berenjak Soho-based modern diner serving Iranian dishes. (p81)

Top Tips for Dining Out

○ Many top-end restaurants offer good value set-lunch menus, giving you the same incredible foodie experience for less.

○ Since the pandemic it's best to book a table for anywhere you really want to eat.

○ Popular restaurants do multiple sittings in a night so your booking may be time-limited.

London on a Plate

The pie: minced beef for purists, but variations allowed

Liquor: a parsley and vinegar sauce; if you don't like the sound of liquor, there's always gravy

Creamy mashed potato, smothered in sauce

★ Top Spots for Pie & Mash

Battersea Pie Station (☎020-7240 9566; www.batterseapie.co.uk; lower ground fl, 28 The Market, Covent Garden; mains £7-10; ⊙11am-7.30pm Mon-Fri, 10am-8pm Sat, 11am-7pm Sun; ⓤCovent Garden)

Goddards at Greenwich (☎020-8305 9612; www.goddardsatgreen wich.co.uk; 22 King William Walk; pie & mash £4.40-8.50; ⊙10am-7.30pm Sun-Thu, to 8pm Fri & Sat; ⓤCutty Sark)

Cockney's Pie and Mash (☎020-8960 9409; www.facebook.com/cockneyspiemashW10; 314 Portobello Rd; pie & mash £3.50; ⊙11.30am-5pm Tue-Sat; ⓤLadbroke Grove or Westbourne Park)

Pie & Mash in London

From the middle of the 19th century until just after WWII, the staple lunch for many Londoners was a spiced-eel pie (eels were once plentiful in the Thames) served with mashed potatoes and liquor. The staple modern-day filling is minced beef (curried meat is also good). Pie-and-mash restaurants are rarely fancy, but they offer something of a time-travel culinary experience.

Goddards at Greenwich

CLAIRE DOHERTY/ALAMY ©

Bar Open

You need only glance at William Hogarth's Gin Lane prints from 1751 to realise that Londoners and alcohol have a colourful history. The metropolis offers a huge variety of venues to wet your whistle – from cosy neighbourhood pubs to thumping all-night clubs and hotel cocktail bars, and all points in between.

Pubs

At the heart of London social life, the pub is one of the capital's great social levellers. Order almost anything you like, but beer is the staple. Some pubs specialise, offering drinks from local microbreweries, fruit beers, organic ciders and other rarer beverages. Others, especially gastropubs, proffer strong wine lists. Some have delightful beer gardens – crucial in summer. Others are exquisitely historic. Most pubs and bars open at 11am, closing at 11pm from Monday to Saturday and 10.30pm on Sunday. Some pubs now have late licences allowing them to stay open past midnight: the 'lock-in' is now a thing of the past, but many Londoners are nostalgic for it.

Bars & Clubs

Bars are generally open later than pubs but close earlier than clubs. They may have DJs and a small dance floor, door charges, more modern decor and fancier (and pricier) drinks, including cocktails. If you're up for clubbing, London has an embarrassment of riches: choose between legendary establishments such as Fabric or smaller clubs with up-and-coming DJs. Dress to impress (no jeans or trainers) or check the dress code online or via social media (fetish clubs require specific outfits, for example). Cocktail bars have experienced a renaissance, as have sober nights out. Expect to see more nonalcoholic drinks, mocktails and CBD-infused options out there.

YUI MOK/PA IMAGES VIA GETTY IMAGES ©

Best Pubs

Lock Tavern Camden pub with roof terrace and live music. (p180)

Lamb Gracefully wreathed in yesteryear loveliness. (p102)

French House Iconic Soho pub with an intelligentsia crowd. (pictured above; p84)

Queen's Arms Tucked down a historic mews near museums and Hyde Park. (p165)

Best Historic Drinking Holes

George Inn History, age-old charm and a National Trust designation. (p142)

Lamb & Flag Atmospheric and creaky old-timer from days of yore, near the Strand. (p83)

Princess Louise Oozing Victorian charm and period panache. (p103)

Gordon's Wine Bar Ancient, underground, candlelit nook off the Strand. (p85)

Best for Cocktails

Lyaness Experimental cocktails in a sumptuous riverfront bar. (p141)

American Bar Stylish Art-Deco gem at the Savoy. (p84)

Nickel Bar Jazz-age vibes in a glamorous Art-Deco foyer. (p123)

Calloh Callay Quirky East London cocktail bar. (p192)

Worth a Trip

Dating from 1585, the **Spaniard's Inn** (p183), near Hampstead Heath, was supposedly highwayman Dick Turpin's hang-out between robberies, but it was also the watering hole for Romantic poets Keats and Byron and artist Sir Joshua Reynolds.

London in a Glass

Strawberries, orange and fresh mint – the bare minimum

One part Pimm's, three parts lemonade

For additional flourish, lemon, lime and cucumber slices

Highball glass (not a pint, this is a classy drink) and ice

★ Top Three Places for Pimm's

Edinboro Castle (p179)

Spaniard's Inn (p183)

Royal Oak (p187)

Pimm's & Lemonade in London

Pimm's, a gin-based fruity spirit, is the quintessential British summer drink: no sunny afternoon in a beer garden would be complete without a glass (or a jug) of it. It is served with lemonade, mint and fresh fruit. Most pubs and bars serve it, although they may only have all the trimmings in summer.

Spaniard's Inn

DAVID SOUTH/ALAMY ©

Treasure Hunt

From charity shop finds to designer labels, there are hundreds of ways to spend in London. Many of the big-name shopping attractions, such as Harrods, Hamleys, Carnaby St and Old Spitalfields Market, are attractions in their own right. If shopping is one of your favourite indulgences, you've come to the right city.

PXL.STORE/SHUTTERSTOCK ©

Major Chain Stores

Major chain stores have taken over shopping centres and high streets, leaving independent shops struggling here too. But they're inexpensive, quick with new looks and conveniently located, so Londoners (and visitors) keep going back for more. As well as familiar global retailers, such as H&M, Urban Outfitters and Zara, you'll spot a few British brands (such as Cath Kidson, Burberry, TOAST, Barbour and Boden).

Opening Hours

London shops generally open from 9am or 10am to 6pm or 7pm, Monday to Saturday. The majority of West End (Oxford St, Soho and Covent Garden), Chelsea, Knightsbridge, Kensington, Greenwich and Hampstead shops also open on Sunday, typically from noon to 5pm or 6pm. Shops in the West End open late (to 9pm) on Thursday; those in Chelsea, Knightsbridge and Kensington open late on Wednesday. Market stalls (like at Camden, Old Spitalfields and Portobello Road) usually start packing up in the late afternoon or as soon as customers dwindle.

Best Shopping Areas

West End Grand confluence of big names for the well heeled and well dressed.

Knightsbridge Harrods and other top names servicing London's wealthiest residents.

Shoreditch and Spitalfields Vintage clothes, makers markets and unique souvenirs.

SHARON WILDIE/SHUTTERSTOCK ©

Best Department Stores

Harrods Garish, stylish and just the right side of kitsch, yet perennially popular. (p166)

Liberty Irresistible blend of contemporary styles in old-fashioned atmosphere. (p87)

Fortnum & Mason London's oldest grocery store, with staff still dressed in tails. (pictured right; p67)

Best Bookshops

John Sandoe Books Knowledgeable customer service and terrific stock. (p167)

Hatchards London's oldest bookshop (1797), with fantastic stock and plenty of events. (p67)

Foyles Once a byword for confusion, now a joy to browse for bibliophiles. (p86)

Libreria Celebrate the printed page in this cultural treasure trove. (p192)

Best for Gifts

Penhaligon's Beautiful range of perfumes and home fragrances. (p67)

Old Spitalfields Market Hand-crafted and hard-to-find pieces from independent traders. (pictured left; p192)

Suck UK Fun, creative gifts you won't want to give away. (p145)

London Fashion Week

The high point on the London fashion calendar is London Fashion Week (www.londonfashionweek.co.uk), held in February and September each year at various venues throughout the city, including Somerset House (p76).

Top London Souvenirs

Music

London is brilliant for vinyl. Try the vintage vinyl shops in Notting Hill, or the iconic Sounds of the Universe (pictured above; p87) for popular and rare finds.

London Toys

Double-decker buses, Paddington bears, guards in bearskin hats: London's icons make for great souvenirs. Hamleys (pictured right; p87) is the place to go.

Tea

The British drink par excellence, with plenty of iconic names to choose from. For lovely packaging to boot, try Fortnum & Mason (pictured left; p67) or Harrods (p166).

Vintage Fashion

Your London vintage clothing and footwear finds will forever be associated with your trip to the city. Start your search at Old Spitalfields Market (p192) or the Sunday Upmarket (p187) in the East End and branch out from there around Brick Lane and its side streets.

Collectable Books

London is heaven for bibliophiles, with numerous history-filled bookshops, brimming with covetable first editions and hard-to-find signed tomes. Get over to Lutyens & Rubinstein (pictured left; p169) or Hatchards (p67).

Show Time

London has been a world leader in the performing arts since a young man from Stratford-upon-Avon set up shop here in the 16th century. An epicentre of alternative culture since the Swinging Sixties, London has something to entertain everyone – whether you're into musicals, opera or fetish club nights, it's here.

Theatre

A night at the theatre is as much a must-do London experience as a trip on the top deck of a double-decker bus. London's Theatreland in the dazzling West End – from Aldwych in the east, past Shaftesbury Ave to Regent St in the west – has a concentration of theatres only rivalled by New York's Broadway.

Classical Music

With multiple world-class orchestras and ensembles, quality venues, reasonable ticket prices and performances covering the musical gamut from traditional crowd-pleasers to innovative compositions, London will satisfy even the fussiest classical-music buffs.

London Sounds

The pandemic impacted London's live music and club scene, but it quickly bounced back. You'll more find music on every night of the week: from cosy dens with experimental, jazz or folk music to major gigs in the many big music venues across the city.

Best Central London Theatres

Donmar Warehouse Intimate space with a diverse, pioneering edge. (p86)

Shakespeare's Globe For the authentic open-air Elizabethan effect. (pictured above; p143)

National Theatre Big productions in a choice of three theatres. (p144)

Best for Classical Music & Opera

Royal Albert Hall Splendid and imposing red-brick Victorian concert hall. (p159)

Royal Opera House Venue of choice for classical ballet and opera buffs. (p85)

COWARDLION/GETTY IMAGES ©

Wigmore Hall Home of international chamber music. (p86)

Best Jazz & Folk

Green Note Intimate live-music venue in Camden. (p180)

Ronnie Scott's Legendary Frith St jazz club in the West End. (p85)

606 Club Long-standing Chelsea basement with a loyal following. (p166)

Best for Rock, Pop, Soul, House, Disco & Electronica

KOKO Former Camden theatre remade. (p180)

Jazz Cafe Despite the name, serves up sounds from all modern genres. (p181)

Scala Live music and club nights in the footsteps of Iggy Pop and Lou Reed. (p103)

Best for Dance Performance

Royal Opera House World-class ballet. (p85)

Southbank Centre From Bollywood to break-dancing,

and all things in between. (p136)

The Place Birthplace of modern English dance. (p104)

Best Churches for Music

Westminster Abbey Even-song and the city's finest organ concerts. (p50)

St Paul's Evensong at its most evocative. (p108)

Discount Tickets

Cut-price standby tickets are an option at some theatres, but apps like Today Tix offer cheap seats ahead of time. Bargain £5 standing-only tickets are available daily at Shakespeare's Globe (p143), but pre-booking is a must.

Museums & Galleries

London's museums and galleries head the list of the city's top attractions, and not just for the rainy days that frequently send locals scurrying for shelter. Some of London's museums and galleries display incomparable collections that make them acknowledged leaders in their field.

ALBERTO ZAMORANO/SHUTTERSTOCK ©

Admission & Access

National museum collections (eg British Museum, National Gallery, and Victoria & Albert Museum) are free, except for temporary exhibitions. Private galleries are usually free (or have a small admission fee), while smaller museums will charge an entrance fee, typically around £10 (book online for discounted tickets at some museums). National collections are generally open 10am to around 6pm, with one late night a week.

Specialist Museums

Whether you've a penchant for fans, London transport, ancient surgical techniques or commercial brands, you'll discover museums throughout the city with their own niche collections. Even for nonspecialists, these museums can be fascinating to browse and to share in the enthusiasm that permeates the collections, tended by their curators.

At Night

Evenings are a great time to visit, as there are fewer visitors. Many museums and galleries open late once a week, and several organise special nocturnal events to extend their range of activities and present the collection in a different mood. Check out museum websites for events, including sleepover opportunities, for both kids and kiddults.

ZGPPHOTOGRAPHY/SHUTTERSTOCK © MILLENNIUM BRIDGE ARCHITECT, NORMAN FOSTER

Best Collections (All Free)

British Museum Supreme collection of rare artefacts and priceless heritage. (p90)

Victoria & Albert Museum Array of decorative arts and design in an awe-inspiring setting. (p148)

National Gallery Tremendous gathering of largely pre-modern masters. (pictured left; p70)

Tate Modern A feast of modern and contemporary art in an equally incredible building. (pictured above; p130)

Natural History Museum A hit with kids and adults alike in one of London's most fabulous buildings. (p152)

Best House Museums

Sir John Soane's Museum Brimming with 18th-century curiosities. (p78)

Dennis Severs' House Home of a Huguenot silk weaver's family, preserved as if still inhabited. (p189)

Apsley House Regency-era home of the Dukes of Wellington. (p160)

Best Small Museums

Old Operating Theatre Museum & Herb Garret Eye-opening foray into old-fashioned surgery techniques. (p138)

Museum of Brands Riveting collection of brand names through the ages. (p169)

Royal College of Music Museum Small collection in a beautiful venue with excellent curation notes. (p161)

Audio Guides

Thanks to COVID-19, most museums no longer have audio guides. You can download dedicated museum apps ahead of time and listen to commentary from your phone. Don't forget your headphones.

Architecture

Waist-deep in history, London's rich seams of eye-opening antiquity appear at every turn. The city's architecture pens a beguiling biography, and a multitude of buildings are instantly recognisable landmarks. There's enough innovation to put a crackle in the air, but it never drowns out London's seasoned and centuries-old narrative.

London Style

Unlike some cities, London has never been methodically planned. Instead, it has developed in a haphazard fashion. As a result, London retains architectural reminders from every period of its long history, but they are often hidden: part of a Roman wall enclosed in the lobby of a modern building near St Paul's Cathedral, say, or a galleried coaching inn from the Restoration in a courtyard off Borough High St.

Best Nicknames

Cheese Grater The 225m-tall Leadenhall Building takes the form of a stepped wedge; it faces architect Richard Rogers' other icon, the Lloyd's of London building.

The Gherkin The 180m-tall bullet-shaped tower that seems to pop up at every turn; aka 30 St Mary Axe. (p124)

Shard Needle-like 87-storey tower by Italian architect Renzo Piano, with awesome views from its top floors. (p137)

Walkie Talkie A 37-storey, 160m-tall tower that bulges in and bulges out. (p118)

The Scalpel A razor-sharp, pointy and angular addition to the ever-shifting city skyline.

Best Early Architecture

Westminster Abbey Titanic milestone in London's ecclesiastical architectural history. (p50)

Houses of Parliament Westminster Hall has one of the finest hammerbeam roofs in the world. (p56)

Tower of London Legend, myth and bloodstained history converge in London's supreme bastion. (p112)

Hampton Court Palace The nation's most impressive and outstanding Tudor edifice. (p200)

ENGEL CHING/SHUTTERSTOCK ©

Best Stately Architecture

Buckingham Palace Central London's royal residence. (p54)

Houses of Parliament Extraordinary Victorian monument and seat of British parliamentary democracy. (p56)

Queen's House Beautiful Inigo Jones Palladian creation in charming Greenwich. (p199)

Hampton Court Palace Get lost in the famous maze or ghost hunt along Tudor hallways. (p200)

Painted Hall Admire this banqueting hall at the Old Royal Naval College. (p199)

Best Monuments

Monument to the Great Fire of London Spiral your way up to panoramic views. (p119)

Albert Memorial Convoluted chunk of Victoriana. (p161)

Wellington Arch Topped by Europe's largest bronze sculpture. (p162)

Open House London

For one weekend at the end of September, hundreds of buildings normally closed to the public throw open their doors for **Open House London** (https://openhouselondon.open-city.org.uk). Public buildings aren't forgotten either, with plenty of talks and tours. This architectural charity sponsors talks with architectural tours held by parent organisation **Open City** (https://open-city.org.uk).

For Kids

IRENE IGNATEVA/SHUTTERSTOCK ©

London is a fantastic place for children. The city's museums will fascinate all ages, and you'll find theatre, dance and music performances ideal for older kids. Playgrounds and parks, city farms and nature reserves are perfect for either toddler energy-busting or relaxation.

Museum Activities

London's museums are very child friendly, with dedicated children or family trails (usually a paper treasure hunt or quiz) in virtually every one. Additionally, you'll find plenty of activities aimed at kids, particularly during British school holidays, including crafts, screenings and pop-up performances. Check on museum websites for specific events.

The Science Museum is one of the most interactive museums for kids, and includes a downstairs area called the Garden aimed at three- to six-year-olds, where tots can splash around (BYO waterproof apron).

Eating with Kids

Many London restaurants and cafes are child-friendly and offer baby-changing facilities and high chairs. Pick your places with some awareness, especially of other diners. Obviously it's best to avoid high-end and quieter restaurants if you have toddlers or babies in tow. Gastro-pubs tend to be pretty family-friendly, especially ones with beer gardens, as are cafes with outdoor spaces. If a children's menu isn't available or your kids are sick of the same children's menu dishes, you can always ask for a starter-sized portion of a main dish.

Best Sights & Activities

ZSL London Zoo Close to 750 species of animals and the excellent Penguin Beach. (p176)

Madame Tussauds Selfie heaven, be it with Harry Styles or Captain Marvel. (p177)

STUDIO MDF/SHUTTERSTOCK ©

Changing the Guard
Soldiers in bearskin hats, red uniforms and military orders: kids will gape. (p64)

London Eye On many bucket lists, from tots to teens. (p136)

Best Museums for Kids

Science Museum Imaginative distractions for technical tykes and a fun-filled basement for little ones. (p158)

London Transport Museum Play among the old Tube carriages and vintage double-decker buses. (p78)

British Museum Meet the mummies at London's best museum. (p90)

Natural History Museum Gawp at the overhanging blue whale skeleton and animatronic T-rex. (p152)

Best for Toddlers & Young Children

Kensington Gardens Fantastic playground in memory of Princess Diana, with a

fountain to splash about in and hectares of greenery. (pictured above; p161)

St James's Park Ducks, squirrels and pelicans. (pictured left; p63)

Hamleys A veritable wonderland awaits in the world's oldest and largest toy shop. (p87)

Family Travel

o Under-11s travel free on all public transport, except National Rail services.

o There's a lack of public toilets in central London. Try www.toiletmap.org.uk for the closest options beyond cafes and pubs, which usually only allow customers in.

Tours

PAUL BICKFORD/SHUTTERSTOCK ©

Best Boat Tours

Thames River Service
(www.thamesriverservices.
co.uk) Cruise boats leave
Westminster Pier for Greenwich, stopping at the Tower
of London.

Thames Rockets (www.
thamesrockets.com) Tear
through London on a high-
speed inflatable boat in
true James Bond fashion.
(pictured left)

Thames River Boats (www.
thamesriverboats.co.uk)
Cruise from Westminster
Pier to the Royal Botanic
Gardens at Kew (1½ hours)
and/or Hampton Court
Palace (another 1½ hours),
with a chance to disembark

at Richmond, if the tide's
right.

Best Bus Tours

Tootbus (www.tootbus.com)
Open-top hop-on, hop-off
bus tours with different
themes, and focused on
sustainability.

Big Bus Tours (www.
bigbustours.com) Informa-
tive commentaries in 12
languages. Ticket includes
a river cruise and three
thematic walking tours.

Best Walking
Tours

Strawberry Tours (www.
strawberrytours.com/
london) Super popular and

operates on a 'pay what
you feel' basis (advertised
as free) on a variety of
themes.

Black History Walks (www.
blackhistorywalks.co.uk)
Learn about London's Black
history through the ages
on these informative tours
and talks.

Guide London (www.
guidelondon.org.uk)
Prestigious and super-
knowledgeable Blue Badge
Tourist Guides who really
know their stuff.

London Walks (www.
walks.com) Large choice
of themed walks to cover
just about any proclivity,
from ghost tours to Beatles,
Harry Potter and Sherlock
Holmes tours.

Under the Radar London

One spot to soak up the best of London local life is at one of the many parks and gardens scattered across the city. Start in the manicured Victoria Park in east London and finish in the expansive wilds of Richmond Park in the west. Park life is where Londoners socialise on a long ramp to admire urban wildlife (wearing stylish wellingtons in winter).

TANIA VOLOSIANKO/SHUTTERSTOCK ©

Park Life

The COVID-19 pandemic deepened London's appreciation for its beautiful green spaces. As with its neighbourhoods, London's parks are plentiful and varied. Join locals admiring flowerbeds in a wrought-iron ringed garden inside a petite square of Georgian terraces, or sitting on a grassy slope watching the sunset behind apartment buildings.

Historic elements blend with modern life in London's parks: you may see a family feeding swans on an ornamental lake, a centuries-old Gothic-style water fountain, or walkers, roller-skaters and cyclists queuing at street-food stalls. On Victoria Park's southern border, a community lives in colourfully painted narrowboats with rooftop gardens. This is the London of everyday life.

Best Parkside Eats

The Magazine, Serpentine North Gallery (www.serpentinegalleries.org) In an extension designed by Zaha Hadid and with a 'climavore' menu, this sun-filled cafe spills out into a hedged green space by Kensington Gardens.

Petersham Nurseries (www.petershamnurseries.com) Pre-book lunch at this Michelin-Green-starred restaurant inside a flower-filled glasshouse before heading to Richmond Park.

Spaniards Inn (www.thespaniardshampstead.co.uk) Grab a Sunday roast at this 16th-century pub with an expansive beer garden opposite Hampstead Heath. (p183)

400 Rabbits (www.400rabbits.co.uk) Serving sourdough pizza and house-made gelato from the lido cafe at Brixton's Brockwell Park.

Pavilion Bakery (www.pavilionbakery.com) Croissants, pastries and an oat-milk coffee are the perfect treats for strolling Victoria Park's broad tree-lined avenue. (pictured above)

London on a Budget

London may be one of the world's most expensive cities, but there are plenty of sights and experiences that are free, or cost next to nothing. Here are some top tips for visiting London on a budget. The permanent collections of taxpayer-funded museums and galleries are open to the public free of charge (although donations are encouraged).

PETRU STAN/SHUTTERSTOCK ©

Best Free Museums & Galleries

National Gallery One of the world's great galleries. (p70)

Victoria & Albert Museum World's largest collection of decorative arts. (p148)

Tate Modern Outstanding modern- and contemporary-art gallery. (p130)

Tate Britain British art from 1500 to the present. (p62)

British Museum UK's most popular museum. (p90)

Science Museum Interactive and educational exhibits. (p158)

Natural History Museum Houses 80 million specimens. (p152)

Best Free Views

Tate Modern Head up to Level 10. (p130)

Sky Garden Book a slot atop the 'Walkie Talkie'. (pictured above; p118)

One New Change Gaze at St Paul's and London. (p122)

Best Budget Theatre

West End theatres Book well ahead for 'limited view' (next to a pillar) or 'limited legroom' (front row of stalls or circle) tickets.

Shakespeare's Globe Find £5 standing-only tickets. (p143)

Best Concerts

St Martin-in-the-Fields Excellent classical music concerts. (p79)

St James's Piccadilly Free lunchtime and evening concerts. (p79)

St Alfege Church In Greenwich. (p199)

Best Walks

Hampstead Heath Roam through North London. (p176)

South Bank Follow the Thames.

West End Walk from A to B.

Best Low-Cost Transport

Santander Cycles Bike-share your way around London. (p84)

Festivals & Events

IVAN YANG/SHUTTERSTOCK ©

London is a vibrant city year-round, celebrating both traditional and modern festivals and events with energy and gusto. From Europe's largest street carnival to the blooms of the Chelsea Flower Show and the pomp and ceremony of Trooping the Colour, London has entrancing and fascinating occasions for all tastes.

Best Free Festivals

Notting Hill Carnival (www.thelondonnottinghillcarnival.com) London's most vibrant outdoor carnival is a celebration of Caribbean London; in August. (pictured above)

Chinese New Year Chinatown fizzes in this colourful street festival in late January or February.

Trooping the Colour June sees parades and pageantry at the Horse Guards Parade off Buckingham Palace.

Guy Fawkes Night (Bonfire Night) Commemorates Guy Fawkes' attempt to blow up parliament in 1605, with bonfires and fireworks on 5 November.

Lord Mayor's Show (www.lordmayorsshow.org) Floats, bands and fireworks to celebrate the Lord Mayor in November.

London Marathon Around 40,000 runners pound through London in April.

Best Ticketed Events

Wimbledon (www.wimbledon.com) Centre of the tennis universe for two weeks in June/July.

The Proms (www.bbc.co.uk/proms) Classical concerts around the Royal Albert Hall from July to September.

London Film Festival (www.bfi.org.uk/lff) Premier film event held at the BFI Southbank and other venues in October.

Chelsea Flower Show (www.rhs.org.uk/chelsea) Renowned horticultural show in May.

New Year On 31 December the countdown to midnight with Big Ben is met with fireworks from the London Eye. Buy tickets for the best view from www.london.gov.uk.

What's On

For a list of events in and around London, check www.visitlondon.com or www.timeout.com/london.

LGBTIQ+ London

The city of Oscar Wilde, Elton John, and the Thames boat-dweller and much-loved comedian and broadcaster Sandi Toksvig won't disappoint queer visitors. There's a fantastic mix of flamboyant, edgy parties and events, plus more sedate bars, pubs and get-togethers year-round. It's a world capital of gaydom, on par with New York and San Francisco.

HELLOTICA/SHUTTERSTOCK ©

By Location

Shoreditch is the epicentre of London's more alternative gay scene, often mixed with the local straight crowd. The long-established gay village of Soho still proudly raises its rainbow flags but has felt the encroachment of gentrification, while Vauxhall hosts the biggest club nights.

Bars & Clubs

Several famous venues closed in recent years – due to rising rents and the pandemic. London still has a varied citywide bar scene.

Best LGBTIQ+ Bars, Clubs & Shops

Royal Vauxhall Tavern (www.vauxhalltavern.com) The UK's best gay cabaret and a major London landmark venue.

Heaven Long-standing club and still a Saturday-night magnet on the gay scene. (p84)

Gay's the Word Excellent range of gay- and lesbian-interest books and magazines. (p105)

Best LGBTIQ+ Events

BFI Flare (www.bfi.org.uk/llgff) Hosted by the BFI Southbank in spring (March/April), with premieres, screenings and talks.

Pride (www.prideinlondon.org) Huge gay pride event in late June/early July (pictured above)

Community Hub

Common Press (www.glasshouse.london) is a bookshop-cafe at the top of Brick Lane, complemented by **Common Counter**, a restaurant and bar serving delicious cocktails , mocktails and craft beers.

Markets

A treasure trove of small designers, unique jewellery, food, original framed photographs and posters, colourful vintage pieces and bric-a-brac, the capital's famed markets are the antidote to shiny carbon-copy shopping centres. Most markets are outdoors, and they are always busy – rain or shine.

I WEI HUANG/SHUTTERSTOCK ©

London Life

Shopping at London's markets isn't just about picking up bargains and rummaging through knick-knacks – although they give you plenty of opportunity to do that. It's also about taking in the character of this vibrant city: Londoners love to trawl through markets, browsing, chatting and socialising.

Lunch on the Side

Food stalls and/or food trucks are a feature of London markets, whether or not the markets specialise in food. The quality varies, but is generally good, and the prices are reasonable (£6 to £10).

Best Markets

Borough Market Bustling cornucopia of gastronomic delights, south of the river. (p136)

Old Spitalfields Market Huge, sprawling market on the border of the City and the East End, excellent for vintage and fashion. (p192)

Camden Market North London's must-see market. (pictured above; p176)

Portobello Road Market London's best-known market, in ever-hip Notting Hill. (p169)

Brick Lane Market Sunday confluence of bric-a-brac, cheap clothes and street eats. (p187)

Sampling Borough Market 🍽

Look out for the plentiful snack samples at Borough Market (p136) south of the river. The quality is top-notch and the variety of flavours breathtaking.

Responsible Travel

Follow these tips when you're in London to leave a lighter footprint, support local and have a positive impact on local communities.

Choose Sustainable

Stay at The Corner, London's greenest hotel where cycling, solar panels, reduced water-use, recycling and chemical-free products are front and centre.

Watch a play at London's carbon-neutral theatre, the Arcola Theatre in Dalston. Not only has it reduced carbon emissions and installed solar panels, but almost all their beers are brewed within a 4 mile radius, reducing transport emissions.

Eat at a pioneering zero-waste restaurant in Hackney Wick. Silo (www. silolondon.com) began with the idea to do away with the rubbish bin. The result: delicious sustainably sourced food.

Go on an Unseen tour (www. unseentours.org.uk) where formerly homeless and socially excluded people earn a living as city guides.

Staying Longer? Give Back

Get fit and give back with the GoodGym (www. goodgym.org), where you run, walk or cycle to do good; help a vulnerable member of society, visit a lonely elder or take part in a community project, all while getting fit.

Volunteer at the Food Cycle (https://foodcycle.org.uk) and turn surplus food into wholesome, nutritious meals for vulnerable Londoners.

Clean up London's canals with London Boaters and Moo Canoes (www.moocanoes. com). Float along the city's

beautiful waterways in a canoe and exchange trash for treats.

Support Local

Visit local street markets to buy from stalls run by locals.

Eat and shop locally. Buy a leather handbag from Paradise Row (paradiserow london.com) made by a local artisan reviving east London's lost leather trade; eat dinner cooked with local ingredients at the Barge East (www. bargeeast.com) restaurant.

Raise a glass to independent brewers. Drink from local microbreweries like the Crate Brewery (https:// cratebrewery.com), Hackney, and the Kernel Brewery (www. thekernelbrewery.com), Bermondsey.

IZABELA HABUR/GETTY IMAGES ©

Learn More

Attend a cultural festival and learn about British-Bangladeshis at the Boishaki Mela.

Visit London neighbour-hoods like Anatolian north London, Afro-Caribbean south London and Bangladeshi east London.

Educate yourself about the history of London's residents at institutes like the Kobi Nazrul Centre (www. https://www.towerhamletsarts.org.uk)and the Black Cultural Archives(www. https://black culturalarchives.org/).

Reduce your Footprint

Shop at zero-waste grocery stores that let you bring your own container.

Use your own shopping bags - you'll be charged otherwise.

Cycle or walk as much as you can when moving around the city.

Buy low-impact clothes and gifts at flea markets and vintage shops.

Take your own 'keep cup' to cafes and coffee shops.

Resources

Trees for Cities (www.treesforcities.org)

HandsOn London (www.handsonlondon.org.uk)

London Wildlife Trust (www.wildlondon.org.uk)

Social Action for Health (www.safh.org.uk)

London Youth (www.londonyouth.org)

Climate Change & Travel

Lonely Planet urges all travellers to engage with their travel carbon footprint. There are many carbon calculators online that allow travellers to estimate the carbon emissions generated by their journey; try www.resurgence.org/resources/carbon-calculator.html.

Four Perfect Days

Day 1

First stop, **Trafalgar Square** (p78) for its architecture and the **National Gallery** (p70) for its superb art. Walk down Whitehall past **Downing St** (p66) to arrive at the **Houses of Parliament** (p56) and **Big Ben**. **Westminster Abbey** (p50) is nearby.

For gourmet cuisine at budget prices, lunch at **Vincent Rooms** (p66). Cross Westminster Bridge to the **London Eye** (pictured above; p136), then stroll South Bank to the **Tate Modern** (p130) for modern art. Admire views of St Paul's from the **Millennium Bridge** (p138) and don't overlook **Shakespeare's Globe** (p143).

Enjoy a drink in **George Inn** (p142) and dinner at **Casa do Frango** (p140) near the historic **Borough Market** (p136).

Day 2

THE PICTURE STUDIO/SHUTTERSTOCK ©

Get to the **Tower of London** (p112) early for the Unlocking of the Tower and follow the beefeaters to marvel at the Crown Jewels. Then admire iconic **Tower Bridge** (pictured above; p120) on the Thames.

Hop on a Tube to **St Paul's** (p108) to explore its architecture and dome and take in the views. Take a bus to **Covent Garden** (p76) to feel the piazza buzz and watch street performers. Continue to **Piccadilly Circus** (p79) and its famous statue and billboards.

Stop by **Dukes London** (p66) for a relaxing martini, followed by Iranian cuisine at **Berenjak** (p81) or Mediterranean at **The Barbary** (p80). Stay in Piccadilly and Soho for cocktails at **Rivoli Bar** (p66), or sink a pint at **Lamb & Flag** (p83).

Day 3

NATURE'S CHARM/SHUTTERSTOCK ©

Spend two hours at the **British Museum** (p90), joining tours of the permanent collection, making time for one of its gallery talks, or exploring on your own. Then stroll around **Bloomsbury**, once the centre of the literary world.

Enjoy a slice of cake at the **London Review Bookshop** (p104) before heading to Chelsea and Kensington to (window) shop. **Harrods** (p166) is a must for gourmet souvenirs, and comb the **Victoria & Albert Museum shop** (p148) too for gifts. End with a stroll around **Hyde Park** (pictured above; p158) or explore the **Natural History Museum** (p152).

Consider dinner at **Launceston Place** (p163), while for drinks the **Queen's Arms** (p165), **K Bar** (p164) or the **Windsor Castle** (p165) are all superb.

Day 4

Take a boat from central London down the Thames to Greenwich, to embark on our **Greenwich walking tour** (p198). Explore the **National Maritime Museum** (p199), **Queen's House** (p199) and the **Cutty Sark** (p199). **Greenwich Market** (pictured above; p199) can sort lunch, with its abundant street food.

Stroll through **Greenwich Park** (p197) up to the **Royal Observatory** (p194). The views unfolding below you to Canary Wharf are magnificent. Inside the observatory, straddle the Greenwich Meridian. Don't overlook the Camera Obscura and, at the Weller Astronomy Galleries, touch something 4.5 billion years old!

Return to the river for a pint and dinner at the picture-postcard **Trafalgar Tavern** (p199).

Need to Know

For detailed information, see Survival Guide (p205)

Language
English

Currency
Pound sterling (£)

Visas
Not required for Australian, Canadian, NZ and US visitors, among others, for stays of up to six months.

Money
ATMs (cashpoints) are widespread. Major credit cards are accepted everywhere.

Mobile Phones
You can buy a local SIM card at the airport.

Time
London is on GMT/UTC.

Tipping
Hotels: £1 per bag. Restaurants: service charge is usually included in bills; otherwise add 10% for decent service. Pubs: never at the bar. Taxis: tips appreciated but not expected.

Daily Budget

Budget: Less than £85
Dorm bed: £20–30
Market-stall lunch or supermarket sandwich: £5–8.50
Museums: many are free
Standby theatre tickets: £5–25
Santander Cycles daily rental fee: £2

Midrange: £85–200
Double room: £100–200
Two-course dinner with a glass of wine: £35
Temporary exhibitions: £12–18
Theatre tickets: £15–60

Top end: More than £200
Four-star or boutique hotel room: from £200
Three-course dinner in top restaurant with wine: £60–90
Black-cab trip: £30
Top theatre tickets: £65

Advance Planning

Three months before Book accommodation, dinner reservations, and tickets for top shows and must-see temporary exhibitions.

One month before Check websites such as Time Out (www.timeout.com/london) for free events, live music and festivals (and book tickets).

A few days before Check the weather forecast online via the Met Office (www.metoffice.gov.uk).

Arriving in London

Most visitors arrive in London by air, or by train from Europe.

✈ From Heathrow Airport

The Tube, including the new Elizabeth Line, costs £12.80. The Heathrow Express (£25) is slightly quicker into Paddington. A taxi or rideshare is £50 to £100.

✈ From Gatwick Airport

Trains to London £12 to £20 (Gatwick Express is quickest); hourly buses to London 24/7 from £10; taxis around £100.

✈ From Stansted Airport

Trains to London cost £20.70; 24/7 buses to London from £15; taxis from £130.

✈ From Luton Airport

Trains to London from £12 to £17; buses 24/7 to London £12; taxis £120.

🚃 From St Pancras International Train Station

Connects to Underground lines to other parts of the city.

Getting Around

The cheapest way to get around London is with an Oyster Card or a UK contactless card (foreign cardholders should check for contactless charges first).

U Tube, Overground & DLR

The London Underground ('the Tube'), Overground and Docklands Light Railway (DLR) are, overall, the quickest ways to get around, if not the cheapest. Selected lines run all night on Friday and Saturday.

🚌 Bus

The bus network is extensive but slow going except for short hops. Fares are good value with an Oyster or contactless cards; there are plentiful night buses and 24-hour routes.

🚗 Taxi

Black-cab fares are steep unless you're in a group. Minicabs are cheaper. Apps such as Gett (for black cabs) and Bolt (minicab) are handy.

🚲 Bicycle

Santander Cycles are ideal for shorter journeys around central London; there are tons of docking stations.

🚗 Car & Motorcycle

As a visitor, it's unlikely you'll need to drive in London. Disincentives include extortionate parking charges, congestion charges, traffic jams, high petrol prices, assiduous traffic wardens and wheel clamps.

London Neighbourhoods

Regent's Park & Camden (p171)
North London has a strong accent on nightlife, parkland and heaths, canal-side charm, markets and international menus.

National Gallery & Covent Garden (p69)
Bright lights, big city: West End theatres, big-ticket museums, fantastic restaurants, shopping galore and boho nightlife.

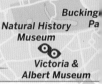

Buckingham Pa

Natural History Museum

Victoria & Albert Museum

Kensington Museums (p147)
One of London's classiest neighbourhoods with fine museums, hectares of parkland and top-grade shopping and dining.

Westminster Abbey & Westminster (p49)
The royal and political heart of London: pomp, pageantry and history in spades, and home to a number of London's biggest attractions.

British Museum & Bloomsbury (p89)

London's most famous museum, elegant squares, eclectic dining and literary pubs.

Shoreditch & the East End (p185)

London's creative and clubbing energy fills Shoreditch with history, museums, ace eats and markets aplenty in the East End.

St Paul's & City of London (p107)

London's iconic church and tower are here, alongside ancient remains, historic churches, architectural gems and hearty pubs.

⊙ St Paul's Cathedral

ish
eum

National Gallery

⊙ Tate Modern

⊙ Tower of London

⊙ Houses of Parliament

stminster
bey

⊙ Royal Observatory & Greenwich Park

Tate Modern & South Bank (p129)

Modern art, innovative theatre, Elizabethan drama, superb dining, cutting-edge architecture and warmly traditional pubs.

Explore
London

Aerial view of London and Tower Bridge (p120)
INGUS KRUKLITIS/SHUTTERSTOCK ©

Explore ◈

Westminster Abbey & Westminster

Westminster is the political heart of London, and the level of pomp and circumstance here is astounding – state occasions are marked by convoys of gilded carriages, elaborate parades and, in the case of the opening of parliament, by a man in a black coat banging on the front door with a jewelled sceptre. Tourists flock here to marvel at Buckingham Palace and the neo-Gothic Houses of Parliament.

The Short List

∘ **Westminster Abbey (p50)** *Admiring London's church for coronations, royal burials and weddings.*

∘ **Buckingham Palace (p54)** *Visiting the monarch's official London residence in summer, or watching the ceremonious Changing the Guard.*

∘ **Houses of Parliament (p56)** *Touring the corridors of power in the spectacular Palace of Westminster.*

∘ **Tate Britain (p62)** *Taking a walk through Britain's artistic heritage.*

∘ **Churchill War Rooms (p62)** *Exploring Britain's underground bunker for WWII strategy.*

Getting There & Around

Ⓤ Westminster and St James's Park are both on the Circle and District Lines. The Jubilee Line runs through Westminster and Green Park; the latter station is also a stop on the Piccadilly and Victoria Lines.

Westminster Abbey & Westminster Map on p60

Houses of Parliament (p56) ALEXEY FEDORENKO/SHUTTERSTOCK ©

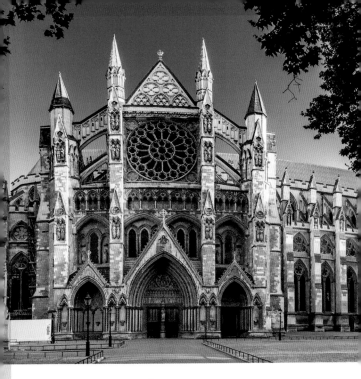

Top Experience 📷
Visit Kings & Queens at Westminster Abbey

Westminster Abbey is such an important commemoration site that it's hard to overstress its symbolic value. Except for Edward V (murdered) and Edward VIII (abdicated), every English sovereign has been crowned here since William the Conqueror in 1066. Sixteen royals have been married here, Queen Elizabeth II's funeral was held here in 2022, and many have been buried here.

◎ MAP P61, E5

www.westminster-abbey.org

20 Dean's Yard

adult/child £24/10

⏱ 9.30am-3.30pm weekdays but to 6pm Wed, to 3pm Sat May-Aug, to 1pm Sat Sep-Apr

Ⓤ Westminster

North Transept, Sanctuary & Quire

The north transept is often referred to as **Statesmen's Aisle**: politicians (notably prime ministers) and eminent public figures are commemorated by large marble statues and imposing marble plaques here. At the heart of the Abbey is the beautifully tiled sanctuary (or sacrarium), a stage for coronations, royal weddings and funerals. The Quire, a magnificent structure of gold, blue and red Victorian Gothic by Edward Blore, dates from the mid-19th century.

Lady Chapel & Coronation Chair

The spectacular Lady Chapel has a fan-vaulted ceiling, colourful heraldic banners and oak stalls. Behind the chapel's altar is the elaborate sarcophagus of Henry VII and his queen, Elizabeth of York. Opposite the entrance to the Lady Chapel is the Coronation Chair, seat of coronation for almost every monarch since the early 14th century.

Tomb of Mary Queen of Scots

There are two small chapels on either side of the Lady Chapel. On the left (north) is where Elizabeth I and her half-sister Mary I (or 'Bloody Mary') rest. On the right (south) is the tomb of Mary Queen of Scots, beheaded on the orders of her cousin Elizabeth in 1587.

Shrine of St Edward the Confessor

The most sacred spot in the abbey lies behind the **High Altar**, where access is generally restricted to protect the 13th-century floor. St Edward was the founder of the Abbey and the original building was consecrated a few weeks before his death. His tomb was slightly altered after the original was destroyed during the Reformation.

★ Top Tips

o Crowds are almost as solid as the Abbey's stonework, so buy tickets online in advance (which also nets a slight discount) or get in the queue first thing in the morning.

o Join one of the 75-minute guided tours for a more in-depth look than the audio guide provides.

o The views from Queen's Diamond Jubilee Galleries are the best in the building.

o Grab something to eat and use the toilet before entering; the cafe and toilets are at the end of the roped route, and it can be hard to get back to where you left off.

✕ Take a Break

Not far from the Abbey, the Vincent Rooms (p66) is an excellent spot for modern European cuisine at reasonable prices. It's operated by the talented hospitality students of Westminster Kingsway College.

Poets' Corner

The south transept contains the Poets' Corner, where many of England's finest writers are buried and/or commemorated. The first poet to be buried here was Geoffrey Chaucer, joined later by Lord Alfred Tennyson, Charles Dickens, Robert Browning, Rudyard Kipling and other greats.

Sir Isaac Newton's Tomb

On the western side of the cloister is the **Scientists' Corner**, where you will find Sir Isaac Newton's tomb. A nearby section of the northern aisle of the nave is known as **Musicians' Aisle**, where baroque composers Henry Purcell and John Blow are buried, as well as more modern music makers such as Benjamin Britten and Edward Elgar.

Cloisters

Providing access to the monastic buildings, the quadrangular Cloisters – dating largely from the 13th to 15th centuries – would have once been a very active part of the Abbey and busy with monks. The Cloisters also provide access to the Chapter House, the Pyx Chamber and the Abbey Museum, situated in the vaulted undercroft.

Chapter House

The octagonal Chapter House has one of Europe's best-preserved medieval tile floors and retains traces of religious murals. Used as a meeting place by the House of Commons in the second half of the 14th century, it also boasts what is claimed to be the oldest door in the UK – it's been there for 950 years.

Pyx Chamber

Next to the Chapter House and off the east cloister, the Pyx Chamber is one of the few remaining relics of the original Abbey and contains the Abbey's treasures and liturgical objects. Note the enormous trunks, which were made inside the room and used to store valuables from the Exchequer.

College Garden

To reach the 900-year-old College Garden (open 10am to 4pm Tuesday to Thursday), enter Little Dean's Yard and the Little Cloisters off Great College St. It occupies the site of the Abbey's first infirmary garden for cultivating medicinal herbs, established in the 11th century.

Queen's Diamond Jubilee Galleries

Opened in 2018, the Queen's Diamond Jubilee Galleries is a museum and gallery space located in the medieval triforium, the arched gallery above the nave. Its exhibits include the death masks of generations of royalty, wax effigies representing Charles II and William III (who is on a stool to make him as tall as his wife, Mary II), armour and stained glass. Highlights are the graffiti-inscribed Mary Chair (used for the coronation of Mary II) and the 13th-century Westminster Retable, England's oldest altarpiece.

History of Westminster Abbey

Although a mixture of architectural styles, Westminster Abbey is considered the finest example of early English Gothic (1190–1300). The original church was built in the 11th century by King (later Saint) Edward the Confessor, who is buried in the chapel behind the High Altar. Henry III (r 1216–72) began work on the new building, but didn't complete it; the French Gothic nave was finished in 1388. Henry VII's huge and magnificent chapel was added in 1519.

Benedictine Monastery & Dissolution

The Abbey was initially a monastery for Benedictine monks. Many of the building's features (the octagonal Chapter House, the Quire and Cloisters) attest to this collegial past. In 1534 Henry VIII separated the Church of England from the Catholic Church and proceeded to dissolve the country's monasteries. The King became head of the Church of England and the Abbey acquired its 'royal peculiar' status (administered directly by the Crown and exempt from any ecclesiastical jurisdiction).

Site of Coronation

With the exception of Edward V and Edward VIII, every English sovereign since William the Conqueror (in 1066) has been crowned here, and most of the monarchs from Henry III (died 1272) to George II (1760) were also buried here.

The Quire

The Quire dates back to the mid-19th century. It sits where the original choir for the monks' worship would have been, but bears little resemblance to the original. Nowadays the Quire is still used for singing, but its regular occupants are the Choir of Westminster Abbey – about 30 boys and 12 'lay vicars' (men) who sing the daily services and evensong (5pm on weekdays except Wednesday and 3pm on weekends).

Royal Wedding

On 29 April 2011 Prince William married Catherine Middleton at Westminster Abbey. The couple had chosen the Abbey for the relatively intimate setting of the Sanctuary –but because of the Quire, three-quarters of the roughly 1900 guests couldn't see a thing! William and Kate's elaborately scrawled marriage certificate is now on display in the Queen's Diamond Jubilee Galleries.

Top Experience 📸
Wave at Royalty at Buckingham Palace

Built in 1703 for the Duke of Buckingham and then purchased by King George III, the palace has been the Royal Family's London lodgings since 1837 when Queen Victoria moved in. Commoners can get a peek at the State Rooms – a mere 19 of the palace's 775 rooms – from mid-July to September when the Royals holiday for the summer.

◎ MAP P60,B4

www.rct.uk/visit/bucking ham-palace

Buckingham Palace Rd

adult/child/under 5yr
£26.50/14.50/free, incl
Royal Mews & Queen's Gallery £49/26.50/free

Ⓤ St James's Park

State Rooms

The tour starts in the Grand Hall at the foot of the Grand Staircase. It takes in John Nash's Italianate Green Drawing Room, the State Dining Room, the Blue Drawing Room (with a fluted ceiling by Nash) and the White Drawing Room, where foreign ambassadors are received.

Picture Gallery & Gardens

The 47m-long Picture Gallery has splendid works by such artists as Van Dyck, Rembrandt, Canaletto, Poussin, Rubens, Canova and Vermeer. Wandering the 16 hectares of gardens after the tour is another highlight, as is admiring some of the 350 or so species of plants.

Queen's Gallery

The royals have amassed a priceless collection of paintings, sculpture, ceramics, furniture and jewellery. The **Queen's Gallery** (www.rct.uk/visit/the-queens-gallery-buckingham-palace) showcases some of these treasures on a rotating basis. Enter from Buckingham Gate.

Royal Mews

Southwest of the palace, the **Royal Mews** (www.rct.uk/visit/royalmews) started life as a falconry but is now a working stable looking after the royals' immaculately groomed horses, along with the opulent vehicles the monarch uses. Highlights include the Gold State Coach of 1762 and the 1911 Glass Coach.

★ Top Tips

o Entry to the palace is by timed ticket (departures every quarter-hour), which must be booked online. The self-guided tour (audio guide included) takes about two hours.

o A **Royal Day Out** is a combined ticket including entry to the State Rooms, Queen's Gallery and Royal Mews.

o The Changing the Guard (p64) is very popular; arrive early to secure a good view.

✗ Take a Break

Head 10 minutes south to the streets around Victoria Station where you'll find a clutch of local pubs, plenty of major chain restaurants from wagamama to Zizzi, plus a handful of fine-diners where bookings and smart casual attire are expected.

Top Experience 📷

Walk the Stately Houses of Parliament

Both the elected House of Commons and the House of Lords, who are appointed or hereditary, sit in the sumptuous Palace of Westminster, a neo-Gothic confection dating from the mid-19th century (with a few sections that survived a catastrophic fire in 1834).

◎ MAP P61, F5

☎ tours 020-7219 4114

www.parliament.uk

Parliament Sq

Ⓤ Westminster

Big Ben

The most famous feature of the Houses of Parliament is the Clock Tower, officially named the Elizabeth Tower to mark Queen Elizabeth II's Diamond Jubilee in 2012 but commonly known as Big Ben. Big Ben is actually the 13.5-tonne bell hanging inside and is named after Benjamin Hall, the first Commissioner of Works when the tower was completed in 1859. It's currently hiding behind scaffolding for restoration works that should be complete by the time you read this.

Westminster Hall

One of the most interesting features of the Palace of Westminster, seat of the English monarchy from the 11th to the early 16th centuries, is Westminster Hall. Originally built at the end of the 11th century, it is the oldest surviving part of the complex; the awesome hammer-beam roof was added between 1393 and 1401.

House of Commons

The House of Commons is where Members of Parliament meet to discuss new legislation and to grill the prime minister and other ministers. The chamber, designed by Giles Gilbert Scott, replaced the one destroyed by a 1941 bomb.

House of Lords

The House of Lords is visited via the amusingly named Strangers' Gallery. The intricate 'Tudor Gothic' interior led its architect, Auguste Pugin (1812–52), to an early death from overwork and nervous strain.

Tours

Visitors are welcome on self-guided or guided tours on Saturdays year-round and on most weekdays during parliamentary recesses. Guided 360-degree tours of the site are available online for free, if you're unable to get inside.

★ Top Tips

o Book tours in advance. Not only are prices cheaper but because they often happen only once a week (on Saturday), but they also fill up quickly.

o Stay for afternoon tea to continue soaking up the splendour.

✕ Take a Break

Head across the river to Southbank Centre for multiple street food options at the Friday-to-Sunday Southbank Centre Food Market, plus a host of British chain restaurants. If you have the time and budget consider booking lunch at the elegant retro-futuristic Skylon (p141) with floor-to-ceiling window views of the Thames and skyline.

Walking Tour 🚶

Royal London

Lassoing the cream of London's royal and stately sights, this attraction-packed walk ticks off some of the city's truly must-do experiences on one comprehensive route. You'll be passing some of London's most famous buildings and historic sites, so photo opportunities abound. The walk conveniently returns you in a loop to your starting point for easy access to other parts of London.

Walk Facts

Start Westminster Abbey;
Ⓤ Westminster

End Houses of Parliament;
Ⓤ Westminster

Length 2.2 miles; two hours

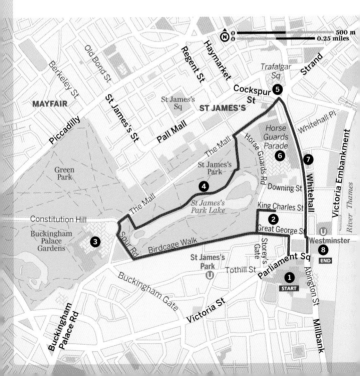

❶ Westminster Abbey

Start by exploring mighty **Westminster Abbey** (p50), preferably before the crowds arrive. Almost every English sovereign since 1066 has been crowned here.

❷ Churchill War Rooms

Walk around Parliament Sq, past the **UK Supreme Court** on the west side of the square, to the **Churchill War Rooms** (p62) to discover how Churchill coordinated the Allied war against Hitler.

❸ Buckingham Palace

Strolling to the end of Birdcage Walk brings you to majestic **Buckingham Palace** (p54), where the State Rooms are accessible to ticket holders in August and September – or pay a visit to the nearby **Royal Mews** (p55) and the **Queen's Gallery** (p55).

❹ St James's Park

Amble along The Mall and enter **St James's Park** (p63), one of London's most attractive royal parks. Walk alongside **St James's Park Lake** for its plentiful ducks, geese, swans and other waterfowl.

❺ Trafalgar Square

Return to The Mall and pass through **Admiralty Arch** to the hubbub of **Trafalgar Square** (p78) and take in the regal views down Whitehall to the Houses of Parliament.

❻ Horse Guards Parade

Walk down Whitehall to the entrance to **Horse Guards Parade** (p64). The dashing mounted sentries of the Household Cavalry are on duty here daily from 10am to 4pm, when the dismounted guards are changed.

❼ Banqueting House

On the far side of the street, magnificent **Banqueting House** (p63) is the last surviving remnant of Whitehall Palace, which vanished in a late-17th-century fire. Further down Whitehall is the entrance to **No 10 Downing Street** (p66).

❽ Houses of Parliament

At the end of Whitehall, you'll reach the magnificently Gothic **Houses of Parliament** (p56) and its famous tower, Big Ben. You can tour the building on a guided or self-directed audio tour or online.

✕ Take a Break

Pack a picnic to eat in lovely **St James's Park** (p63) if it's a sunny day. Alternatively, **Cafe Murano** (www.cafemurano. co.uk) in the nearby neighbourhood of St James's is a fine choice for authentic and delicious cuisine from northern Italy, especially the two- or three-course set lunch menu.

F
200 m
0.1 miles
Villiers St
Charing Cross
Craven St
Strand
Embankment
Golden
Jubilee
Bridges
Northumberland Ave
1
2
Whitehall Ct
Whitehall
Horse Guards Ave
Banqueting
6 House
Victoria Embankment
Richmond Tce
Westminster
Whitehall
Parliament Sq
Westminster
Bridge
Parliament St
3
4

E
Trafalgar
Sq
Whitehall
Spring Gdns
Cockspur St
Horse
Guards
Parade
8
No 10
Downing
Street
Downing St
Horse Guards Rd
King Charles St
Churchill
War Rooms 2
Great George St
Old Queen St

D
Suffolk St
Haymarket
St Alban's St
Regent St
ST JAMES'S
Charles II St
Carlton House Tce
Carlton Gdns
The Mall
St James's
Park Lake
St James's
Park 5
Birdcage Walk

C
Jermyn St
Ormond
Yard
Eagle St
St James's
Sq
King St
Duke St
Pall Mall
St James's St
Cleveland
Row
Marlborough Rd
Spur Rd

B
Royal
Academy
of Arts
16
4 3
14 15
17
Piccadilly
Burlington
Arcade
New Bond St
Albemarle St
Dover St
Café
Murano
13
9
St James's St
Bury St
Park Pl
St James's St 12
Queen's Walk
Green
Park
Changing
the Guard
7
Constitution Hill
Buckingham
Palace

A
10
Curzon St
Berkeley St
Piccadilly

1
2
6
3
4

N

Westminster Abbey & Westminster

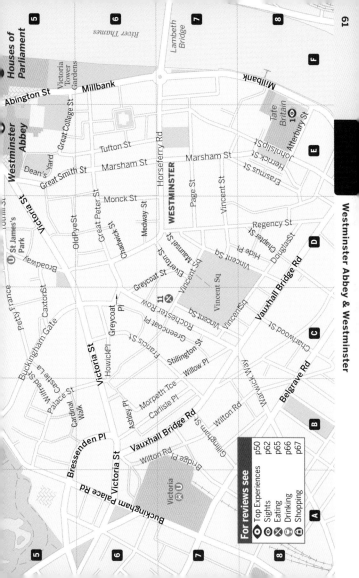

Houses of
Parliament

5

River Thames

6

Lambeth
Bridge

7

Millbank

8

F

Victoria
Tower
Gardens

Millbank

Abington St

Tate
Britain ❶

Atterbury St

E

Westminster
Abbey

Great College St

Johnsfords St

Herrick St

Erasmus St

Tufton St

Dean's Yard

Great Smith St

Marsham St

Horseferry Rd

Page St

Marsham St

Vincent St

WESTMINSTER

Monck St

Great Peter St

Medway St

Chadwick St

Old Pye St

Regency St

Chapter St

Douglas St

Hide Pl

Vincent Sq

D

Victoria St

St James's
Park Ⓤ

Broadway

Caxton St

Greycoat St

Elverton St

Maunsel St

Vincent Sq

Vincent Sq

Vincent St

Vauxhall Bridge Rd

Charlwood St

C

Petty France

Buckingham Gate

Greycoat Pl

Greencoat Pl

Rochester Row

❶❶ ✕

Francis St

Stillington St

Willow Pl

Warwick Way

Wilfred St

Castle La

Palace St

Cardinal Walk

Howick Pl

Morpeth Tce

Carlisle Pl

Ashley Pl

Victoria St

Vauxhall Bridge Rd

Wilton Rd

Belgrave Rd

B

Bressenden Pl

Victoria St

Gillingham St

Bridge Pl

Wilton Rd

Buckingham Palace Rd

Victoria Ⓤ Ⓡ

A

8

For reviews see	
◉ Top Experiences	p50
◉ Sights	p62
✕ Eating	p65
🍷 Drinking	p66
🛍 Shopping	p67

Sights

Tate Britain

GALLERY

1 ⊙ MAP P61, E8

On the site of the former Millbank Penitentiary, the older and more venerable of the two Tate siblings opened in 1892 and celebrates British art from 1500 to the present, including pieces from William Blake, William Hogarth, Thomas Gainsborough and John Constable, as well as vibrant modern and contemporary pieces from Lucian Freud, Barbara Hepworth, Gillian Ayres, Francis Bacon and Henry Moore. The stars of the show are, undoubtedly, the light-infused visions of JMW Turner in the Clore Gallery. (www.tate.org.uk/visit/tate-britain)

Churchill War Rooms

MUSEUM

2 ⊙ MAP P60, E4

Former Prime Minister Winston Churchill helped coordinate the Allied resistance against Nazi Germany on a Bakelite telephone from this underground complex during WWII. The **Cabinet War Rooms** remain much as they were when the lights were switched off in 1945, capturing the drama and dogged spirit of the time, while the modern multimedia **Churchill Museum** affords intriguing insights into the life and times of the resolute, cigar-smoking wartime leader. (www.iwm.org.uk/visits/churchill-war-rooms)

Royal Academy of Arts

GALLERY

3 ⊙ MAP P60, B1

Britain's oldest society devoted to fine arts was founded in 1768 and moved here to Burlington House a century later. For its 250th birthday in 2018, the RA gave itself a £56-million makeover. Its collection of drawings, paintings, architectural designs, photographs and sculptures by past and present Royal Academicians, such as Sir Joshua Reynolds, John Constable, Thomas Gainsborough, JMW Turner, David Hockney and Tracey Emin, has historically been male-dominated, but this is slowly changing. (www.royalacademy.org.uk)

Burlington Arcade

HISTORIC BUILDING

4 ⊙ MAP P60, B1

Flanking Burlington House, which is home to the Royal Academy of Arts, is this delightful arcade, built in 1819. Today it is a shopping precinct for the wealthy, and is most famous for the Burlington Beadles, uniformed guards who patrol the area keeping an eye out for such offences as running, chewing gum, whistling, opening umbrellas or anything else that could lower the tone. (The fact that the arcade once housed a brothel is best left unsaid.)

Running perpendicular to it between Old Bond and Albermarle Sts is the more recent 1880 **Royal Arcade**. (www.burlingtonarcade.com)

St James's Park

PARK

5 ⊙ MAP P60, C3

At 23 hectares, St James's is the second-smallest of the eight royal parks after **Green Park** (www.royalparks.org.uk/parks/green-park). But what it lacks in size it makes up for in grooming, as it is the most manicured green space in London. It has brilliant views of the London Eye, Westminster, St James's Palace, Carlton House Terrace and Horse Guards Parade; the picture-perfect sight of Buckingham Palace from the **Blue Bridge** spanning the central lake is the best you'll find. (www.royalparks.org.uk/parks/st-jamess-park)

Banqueting House

PALACE

6 ⊙ MAP P60, F3

Banqueting House is the sole surviving section of the Tudor Whitehall Palace (1532) that once stretched most of the way down Whitehall before burning to the ground in a 1698 conflagration. Designed by Inigo Jones in 1622 and refaced in Portland stone in the 19th century, Banqueting House was England's first purely Renaissance building and resembled no other structure in the country at the time. Don't miss **The Undercroft** cellar. (www.hrp.org.uk/banqueting-house)

Burlington Arcade

Changing the Guard CEREMONY

7 ⊙ MAP P60, B4

The full-on pageantry of soldiers in bright-red uniforms and bearskin hats parading down the Mall and into Buckingham Palace (p54) is madly popular with tourists. The event lasts about 45 minutes and ends with a full military band playing music from traditional marches, musicals and pop songs. The pomp and circumstance can feel far away indeed when you're in a row 15, trying to watch the ceremony through a forest of selfie sticks. Get here at least 45 minutes before the main event. (www.royal.uk/changing-guard)

Horse Guards Parade HISTORIC SITE

8 ⊙ MAP P60, E3

In a more accessible version of Buckingham Palace's Changing the Guard, the horse-mounted troops of the Household Cavalry swap soldiers here at 11am from Monday to Saturday and at 10am on Sunday. A slightly less ceremonial version takes place at 4pm when the dismounted guards are changed. The **Trooping the Colour** (www.householddivision.org.uk/trooping-the-colour) parade takes place here in June.

Trooping the Colour

LONNDUBH/SHUTTERSTOCK ©

Queen Elizabeth II

On Thursday 8 September 2022, the longest-serving British monarch, Queen Elizabeth II, died aged 96. Elizabeth came to the throne back in 1952 at the age of 27, reigning over the Commonwealth for 70 years. She was often described as a stabilising force for Britain during a period of considerable global and social change.

Elizabeth died at her much-loved Scottish estate, Balmoral, 17 months after the death of her husband Prince Philip. In the week that followed, while the nation was in official mourning and many major events were cancelled, the Queen's coffin was transported to London, via Edinburgh. A state funeral was held at Westminster Abbey followed by a private ceremony at St George's Chapel in Windsor where the Queen is now buried with Philip.

The Queen's stoic (and socially distanced) presence at the royal ceremonial funeral for her companion of seven-plus decades, during the height of the coronavirus pandemic in April 2021, was one of the enduring images of that period.

On the Saturday following the Queen's death, Charles was officially proclaimed King Charles III. His second wife, Camilla, became the Queen Consort of the United Kingdom.

Eating

Kitty Fisher's   MODERN BRITISH £££

9 ⊗ MAP P60, A2

Taking pride of place in Mayfair's 18th-century Shepherd Market (historically one of London's red-light districts), this cosy dining room is named after the 18th-century courtesan painted by Joshua Reynolds. Now a handsomely furnished, twin-roomed restaurant, it serves quality British fare such as monkfish with cauliflower and curried butter, or pork chops with salsa verde, pickled raisins and chicory. The wine list and cocktail names are also excellent. (www.kittyfishers.com)

Briciole   ITALIAN ££

10 ⊗ MAP P60, A1

'Crumbs' is an inviting corner trattoria with a cafe and deli out the front and a cosy dining room out the back. The food isn't overly complex: Palermo-style meatballs, braised lamb shank with polenta, and plenty of pasta. But, of course, simplicity and deliciousness are the cornerstones of real Italian fare, and the prices are reasonable. (http://briciole.co.uk)

No 10 Downing St

The official office of British leaders since 1735, when George II presented No 10 to 'First Lord of the Treasury' Robert Walpole, **No 10 Downing St** (www.number10.gov. uk) has also been the prime minister's London residence since refurbishment in 1902. For such a famous address, No 10 is a small-looking Georgian building on a plain-looking street, hardly warranting comparison with the White House, for example. Yet it is actually three houses joined into one and boasts roughly 100 rooms plus a 2000-sq-metre garden.

Vincent Rooms

MODERN EUROPEAN **££**

11 🍴 MAP P61, C7

Care to be a guinea pig for student chefs at Westminster Kingsway College, where such celebrity chefs as Jamie Oliver and Ainsley Harriott were trained? Service is eager to please, the atmosphere in both the Brasserie and the Escoffier Room smarter than expected, and the food (including veggie options) ranges from wonderful to exquisite – at very affordable prices. (www.thevincentrooms.co.uk)

Drinking

Dukes London

COCKTAIL BAR

12 🚇 MAP P60, B2

Superb martinis and a gentlemen's-club-like ambience are the ingredients of this classic bar, where white-jacketed masters mix up perfect preparations. James Bond fans should make a pilgrimage here: author Ian Fleming used to frequent the place, where he undoubtedly ordered his drinks 'shaken, not stirred'. Smokers can ease into the secluded Cognac and Cigar Garden to enjoy cigars purchased here. (www.dukeshotel.com/dukes-bar)

Rivoli Bar

COCKTAIL BAR

13 🚇 MAP P60, B2

You may not quite need a diamond as big as the **Ritz** (www.theritz london.com) to drink at this Art-Deco marvel, but it might help. All camphor wood, illuminated Lalique glass, golden-ceiling domes and stunning cocktails, the bar is a gem. Unlike in some other parts of the Ritz, the dress code here is smart casual (although trainers are not permitted).

Caviar, oysters, and more substantial classics such as lobster rolls and club sandwiches (£32 to £750) are available between 11.30am and 10.30pm. (www.theritz london.com/dine-with-us/rivoli-bar)

Shopping

Fortnum & Mason
DEPARTMENT STORE

4 🔒 MAP P60, B1

With its classic eau-de-nil (pale green) colour scheme, the 'Queen's grocery store' (established in 1707) refuses to yield to modern times. Its staff – men and women – still wear old-fashioned tailcoats, and its glamorous food hall is supplied with hampers, marmalade and speciality teas. Stop for a spot of afternoon tea at the **Diamond Jubilee Tea Salon**, visited by Queen Elizabeth II in 2012. (www.fortnumandmason.com)

Hatchards
BOOKS

5 🔒 MAP P60, C1

The UK's oldest bookshop dates from 1797, and has been cramped into this five-storey Georgian building for more than 200 years. Holding three royal warrants, Hatchards has a solid supply of signed editions and first editions on the ground floor. (www.hatchards.co.uk)

Penhaligon's
PERFUME

6 🔒 MAP P60, B1

Follow your nose through the historic Burlington Arcade (p62) to this classic British perfumery. Attendants enquire about your

Westminster Nightlife?

Westminster and Whitehall are fairly deserted in the evenings, with little in the way of bars or restaurants. It's pretty much the same story for St James's. Instead, head north to Soho for a vibrant concentration of bars, restaurants and live music, or across the Thames to South Bank's theatres, pubs and restaurants.

favourite smells, take you on an exploratory tour of the shop's signature range, and help you discover new scents in their traditional perfumes, home fragrances, and bath and body products. Everything is produced in England, with prices to match. (www.penhaligons.com)

Paxton & Whitfield
FOOD & DRINKS

17 🔒 MAP P60, C1

With modest beginnings as an Aldwych stall in 1742 and purveying a dizzying range of fine cheeses, this black-and-gold-fronted shop holds two royal warrants. Whatever your cheese leanings, you'll find the shop well supplied with hard and soft cheeses as well as blue and washed-rind examples. (www.paxtonandwhitfield.co.uk)

Explore ⊕
National Gallery & Covent Garden

At the centre of the West End – London's physical, cultural and social heart – the neighbourhood around the National Gallery and Covent Garden is a sightseeing hub. This is London's busiest neighbourhood, with a grand convergence of monumental history, stylish restaurants, standout entertainment choices and classic pubs. And if you're in town to shop, you'll be in seventh heaven.

The Short List

◦ **National Gallery (p70)** *Admiring masterpieces from Europe in this palatial gallery.*

◦ **Somerset House (p76)** *Viewing a high-profile art gallery, or ice skating in winter.*

◦ **Covent Garden Piazza (p76)** *Eating, drinking and being merry in a bustling piazza.*

◦ **Soho (p77)** *Strolling London's most infamous streets for eating, drinking and partying.*

◦ **Foyles (p86)** *Enjoying fantastic shopping, from stellar bookshops like this one to high-fashion and vinyl stores.*

Getting There & Around

U Alight at Piccadilly Circus, Leicester Sq and Covent Garden (all on the Piccadilly Line), or Leicester Sq, Charing Cross and Embankment (all on the Northern Line).

National Gallery & Covent Garden Map on p74

National Gallery (p70-1) JEFF WHYTE/SHUTTERSTOCK ©

Top Experience 📷
Review European Art History at the National Gallery

With some 2,300 European paintings on display, this is one of the world's richest art collections, with seminal paintings from the mid-13th to the early 20th century, including works by Leonardo da Vinci, Michelangelo, Titian, Van Gogh and Renoir.

◉ MAP P75, E6

www.nationalgallery.org.uk

Trafalgar Sq

admission free

🕐 11am-6pm Sat-Thu, to 9pm Fri

Ⓤ Charing Cross

Renaissance

The Sainsbury Wing (1260–1510, rooms 51 to 66) houses plenty of fine religious paintings commissioned for private devotion, as well as more unusual masterpieces such as Botticelli's *Venus & Mars*. Leonardo da Vinci's *Virgin of the Rocks* (room 66) is a visual and technical masterpiece.

High Renaissance & Baroque

Works from the High Renaissance (1500–1600) embellish rooms 9 to 14 where Michelangelo, Titian, Raphael, Correggio, El Greco and Bronzino hold court; Rubens, Rembrandt and Caravaggio grace rooms 15 to 32 (1600–1700). Notable are two self-portraits of Rembrandt in room 22 and the *Rokeby Venus* by Velázquez in room 30.

Neo-classicism to Impressionism

Rooms 33 to 45 (1700–1930) are the main attraction for many visitors: they have works by 18th-century British artists such as Gainsborough, Constable and Turner, and seminal Impressionist and post-Impressionist masterpieces by Van Gogh, Renoir and Monet.

Rain, Steam & Speed: The Great Western Railway

In room 34, this magnificent oil painting from Turner was created in 1844. Generally considered to depict the Maidenhead Railway Bridge, the painting reveals the forces reshaping the world at the time: railways, speed and a reinterpretation of the use of light, atmosphere and colour in art. Look for the dashing hare.

Sunflowers

In room 43 hangs one of several sunflower still lifes painted by Van Gogh in late 1888; this masterpiece – which hangs next to *Van Gogh's Chair*, another masterpiece – displays a variety of then-innovative artistic techniques.

★ **Top Tips**

o Free one-hour guided tours leave from the Sainsbury Wing foyer at 3pm Tuesday to Thursday.

o If you want to go it alone, download the Smartify app for an audio guide.

o The gallery is open until 9pm on Friday.

✕ **Take a Break**

Historic Gordon's Wine Bar (p85) nearby serves cheese platters with its wines inside the cavernous candlelit interior or at sunny tables on Watergate Walk.

For something fancier, head to Barrafina (p83) for top-notch tapas and other delectable Spanish fare.

Walking Tour 🚶

A Stroll Through Soho

Soho may come into its own in the evenings, but daytime guarantees other surprises and opportunities to be charmed by the area's bohemian leanings, history, diversity and creative energy. Thread your way from Chinatown through intriguing backstreets, genteel squares and markets to one of the neighbourhood's signature bars.

Walk Facts

Start Chinatown;
Ⓤ Leicester Sq

Finish French House;
Ⓤ Leicester Sq

Length 1.2 miles; three to six hours

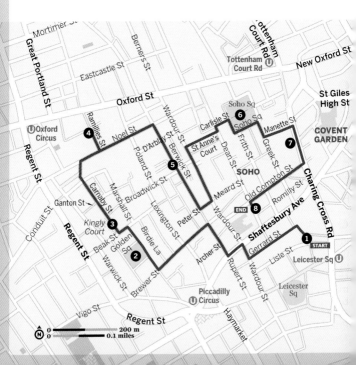

❶ Chinatown

Just north of Leicester Sq Tube station are Lisle and Gerrard Sts, focal points for London's Chinese community. A tight tangle of supermarkets, roast-duck shops and dim-sum canteens, it's a vibrant spot for a bite to eat and drink.

❷ Golden Square

North of Brewer St, historic Golden Sq (featured in Charles Dickens' *The Life and Adventures of Nicholas Nickleby*) was once part of an area called Windmill Fields. This lovely 17th-century square was probably Christopher Wren's design. The garden in the middle is a relaxing place popular with the local office crowd.

❸ Carnaby Street

Synonymous with the Swinging Sixties, London's subcultures have always congregated around Carnaby St. Today its colourful facades house an eclectic mix of designer and big-name brand stores. Between its street art and themed Christmas lights, it's hugely photogenic.

❹ Photographers' Gallery

Inspiring **Photographers' Gallery** (https://thephotographersgallery.org.uk) has five floors of exhibition space, a cafe and a shop brimming with prints and photography books. It awards the prestigious Deutsche Börse Photography Prize, of considerable importance for contemporary photographers.

❺ Berwick Street

The vinyl revival is alive and well in neighbouring Berwick and Broadwick Sts. With some of London's best music shops, you'll be riffling through excellent back catalogues across genres from rock to soul, reggae and dubstep.

❻ Soho Square

Cut through tiny St Anne's Court to Dean St (where Karl Marx lived at No 28 between 1851 and 1856) and leafy **Soho Square** (p77), where Londoners catch some sun on uncloudy days. Laid out in 1681, it was originally named King's Square (hence the statue of Charles II).

❼ Foyles

Is there a better way to while away an afternoon than at a bookshop? **Foyles** (p86), London's legendary bookshop, sells titles on every topic imaginable plus Grant & Cutler foreign-language titles on the 4th floor; an excellent cafe is on the 5th.

❽ French House

Walk down Old Compton St to Soho's legendary boozer, **French House** (p84), the meeting place of Free French Forces during WWII – de Gaulle is said to have drunk here, while Dylan Thomas, Peter O'Toole and Francis Bacon often ended up horizontal.

1

24

33

All Saints **13**
Margaret
Street

Mortimer St

Riding Wells St

Margaret St

Eastcastle St

Winsley St

Newman St

Berners St

Great Russell St

Bedford Ave

Gresse St

Hanway St

Rathbone Pl

Tottenham Court Rd

Tottenham Court Rd

2

Oxford St

Sutton Row

Poland St

Ramillies St

Noel St

Great Chapel St

Soho Sq

Soho Sq

Frith St

Manette St

Denman St

Charing Cross Rd

26

Great Marlborough St

D'Arblay St

Berwick St

St Anne's Ct

Dean St

Greek St

35

3

41

17

Poland St

Broadwick St

Berwick St Market

Ingestre Pl

Wardour St

Meard St

Soho **4**

31

16

Old Compton St

38

40

37

Regent St

Ganton St

Marshall St

Carnaby St

Beak St

Lexington St

Peter St

28

SOHO

4

Golden Sq

Birdie La

Great Windmill St

Archer St

Shaftesbury Ave

Chinatown
Gate

Gerrard St

Lisle St

Wardour St

Leicester Pl

Princ
Char
Ciner

18

Brewer St

Sherwood St

Denman St

Rupert St

5

Savile Row

Heddon St

Warwick St

Glasshouse St

**Piccadilly
Circus**

10

Piccadilly
Circus

Jermyn St

Oxendon St

Panton St

St Martin's St

LEICESTER
SQUARE

5

Burlington Gardens

Sackville St

Regent St

Eagle Pl

St Alban's St

Haymarket

Whitcomb St

6

Old Bond St

Burlington Arcade

Piccadilly

11

St James's
Piccadilly

Duke of York St

Jermyn St

ST JAMES'S

Charles II St

Regent St

Charles II St

Charles II St

Suffolk St

Pall Mall

Cockspu

200 m
0.1 miles

E **F** **G** **H**

Bloomsbury St

Great Russell St

Museum St

Bloomsbury Way

Southampton Row

Southampton Pl

High Holborn

HOLBORN **1**

Ⓤ Holborn

Whetstone Park

7 ◉

New Oxford St

High Holborn

Newton St

Lincoln's Inn Fields

Sir John Soane's Museum

Gate St

Lincoln's Inn Fields **2**

Bucknall St

Grape St

Drury La

Stukely St

Macklin St

Parker St

Great Queen St

Kingsway

St Giles High St

Endell St

Shorts Gardens

Betterton St

Shelton St

COVENT GARDEN

Wild Ct

Wild St

9 ◉

19 ◉

St Giles-in-the-Fields

Neal St

15 ◉

39 🔒 ◉

22 ◉

34 ◉

Earlham St

Shaftesbury Ave

New Compton St

Long Acre

Broad Ct

Drury La

Crown Ct

Russell St

Kemble St

Kean St

Tavistock St

Aldwych

21 ◉ **3**

Flower Market

Neal St

Langley St

36 🔒

Mercer St

Long Acre

Floral St

Covent Garden

James St

Covent Garden St

King St

32 ◉

Bow St

London Transport Museum

3 ◉ **8** ◉

Wellington St

Exeter St

Tavistock St

Strand **4**

West St

Monmouth St

Rose St

25 ◉

Garrick St

Covent Garden Piazza

St Paul's Church

Henrietta St

Maiden La

Southampton St

Carting La

Savoy St

14 ◉

Somerset House

1 ◉

Ⓤ Leicester Sq

New Row

St Martin's La

Bedfordbury

Chandos Pl

27 ◉

20 ◉

Charing Cross Rd

National Portrait Gallery **2** ◉

National Gallery ◉

12 ◉

St Martin-in-the-Fields

William IV St

23 ◉

Strand

John Adam St

Adam St

Savoy Pl

Victoria Embankment **5**

6 ◉

Trafalgar Square

Villiers St

29 ◉

30 ◉

Victoria Embankment Gardens

Craven St

Charing Cross

Ⓤ

Ⓤ Embankment

Whitehall

Northumberland Ave

For reviews see		
◉ Top Experiences	p70	
◉ Sights	p76	
✕ Eating	p80	
◔ Drinking	p83	
✿ Entertainment	p85	
🔒 Shopping	p86	

E **F** **G** **H**

6

Sights

Somerset House

HISTORIC BUILDING

1 ◉ MAP P75, H4

Designed in 1775 for government departments and royal societies – perhaps the world's first office block – Somerset House now contains galleries, restaurants and cafes that encircle a lovely open courtyard and extend to an elevated sun-trap terrace. The stand-out attraction is the **Courtauld Gallery**, which hosts a small but exceptional Impressionist collection. The **Embankment Galleries** are devoted to temporary exhibitions (usually photography, design or fashion). The grand courtyard hosts a range of events year-round, including an atmospheric ice-skating rink in winter. (www.somersethouse.org.uk)

National Portrait Gallery

GALLERY

2 ◉ MAP P75, E5

What makes the National Portrait Gallery so compelling is its familiarity; in many cases, you will have heard of the subject (royals, scientists, politicians, celebrities) or the artist (Andy Warhol, Annie Leibovitz, Lucian Freud), but you won't necessarily recognise the face. The gallery is closed until spring 2023 for a major refurbishment, which will see new public and exhibition space. (www.npg.org.uk)

Covent Garden Piazza

LANDMARK

3 ◉ MAP P75, G4

London's wholesale fruit-and-vegetable market until 1974 is now mostly the preserve of visitors, who flock here to shop among the quaint Italian-style arcades, eat and drink in the myriad cafes and restaurants, browse through eclectic market stalls in the Apple Market, toss coins at street performers on the West Piazza and traipse through the fun London Transport Museum (p78). Note that the shops are becoming increasingly high-end, with couture houses such as Chanel and Dior opening shop in the market building.

The open square in front of **St Paul's Church** (http://actorschurch.org), nicknamed the Actors' Church, has long been a place of performance: even Samuel Pepys' diary from 1662 mentions an Italian puppet play with a character named Punch. The best views of the action today are from the upper terrace of **Punch & Judy** pub. An old painted **noticeboard** with rules and charges for vendors can still be found lurking in one of the alleys on the northern side, and black-and-white photos of Covent Garden's days as a food traders' market line the walls of the narrow passages. The kitsch is hauled out for the quirky **Rent Ceremony**, in which the chairman and trustees strut around the piazza, accompanied by a town crier and live band, to pay Covent Garden's landlord the yearly rent of five red apples and five posies of flowers. It usually takes place in June. (www.coventgarden.london)

Soho   AREA

4  ⊙ MAP P74, D3

In a district that was once pasture-land, the name Soho is thought to have evolved from a hunting cry. While the centre of London nightlife has shifted east, the neighbourhood definitely comes into its own in the evenings and remains a proud gay district. You'll be charmed by the area's vitality during the day too.

At Soho's northern end, leafy **Soho Sq** (Ⓤ Tottenham Court Rd or Leicester Sq) is the area's back garden. It was laid out in 1681 and originally called King's Sq; a statue of Charles II stands in its northern half. In the centre is a tiny half-timbered mock-Tudor cottage built as a gardener's shed in the 1870s. The space below it was used as an underground bomb shelter during WWII.South of the square is **Dean St**, lined with bars and restaurants. No 28 was the home of Karl Marx and his family from 1851 to 1856; they lived here in extreme poverty as Marx researched and wrote *Das Kapital* in the Reading Room of the British Museum.**Old Compton St** is the epicentre of Soho's gay village. It's a street loved by all, gay or otherwise, for its great bars, risqué shops and general good vibes.Seducer and heart-breaker Casanova and opium-addicted writer Thomas de Quincey lived on nearby **Greek St**, while the parallel

Historic Dean Street

Frith St housed Mozart at No 20 for a year from 1764.

Chinatown Gate   LANDMARK

5 ⊙ MAP P74, D4

Northwest of Leicester Sq but a world away in atmosphere, this grand tile-roofed and red-pillared gate marks the entrance into Chinatown. Although not as big as Chinatowns in other world-class cities – it's just Lisle and Gerrard Sts, really – London's version is a lively quarter with street signs in Chinese script, red lanterns strung up across the streets bobbing in the breeze, and restaurants, noodle shops and Asian supermarkets crammed in cheek by jowl.

The quality of food varies enormously, but there's a good choice of places for dim sum and other cuisines from across China and other parts of Asia. There are smaller, more 'Westernised' gates at both ends of Gerrard St and on Macclesfield St too. To see the area at its effervescent best, time your visit for **Lunar New Year** in late January or early February. London's original Chinatown was at Limehouse in the East End but moved here after heavy bombardments in WWII. (www. chinatown.co.uk)

Trafalgar Square   SQUARE

6 ⊙ MAP P75, E6

Opened to the public in 1844, Trafalgar Sq is the true centre of London, where rallies and marches take place, tens of thousands of revellers usher in the New Year and locals congregate for anything from communal open-air cinema and Christmas celebrations to political protests. It is dominated by the 52m-high **Nelson's Column**, guarded by four **bronze lion statues**, and ringed by many splendid buildings, including the National Gallery (p70) and the church of St Martin-in-the-Fields (p79).

Sir John Soane's Museum   MUSEUM

7 ⊙ MAP P75, H1

This museum is one of the most atmospheric and fascinating in London. The Georgian building was the beautiful, bewitching home of architect Sir John Soane (1753–1837), which he bequeathed to the nation through an Act of Parliament on condition that it remain untouched after his death and free to visit. It's brimming with Soane's vast collection of art and archaeological purchases, as well as intriguing personal effects and curiosities. The house-museum represents his exquisite and eccentric tastes, persuasions and proclivities. (www.soane.org)

London Transport Museum   MUSEUM

8 ⊙ MAP P75, G4

Housed in Covent Garden's former flower-market building, this captivating museum looks at how London developed as a result of better transport. It's stuffed full of horse-drawn omnibuses, vintage Underground carriages with heritage maps, and old double-decker buses (some of which you can clamber through, making this something of a kids' playground). The gift shop sells great London souvenirs such as retro Tube posters and pillows made from the same fabric as the train seats. (www.ltmuseum.co.uk)

Lincoln's Inn   HISTORIC BUILDING

9 ◉ MAP P75, H2

The attractive Lincoln's Inn has a chapel with lovely stained glass, a pleasant square and picturesque gardens that invite a stroll, especially early or late in the day. Although the Great Hall is closed to the public, it is visible through the gates and is relatively intact, with original 15th-century buildings, including the Tudor Lincoln's Inn Gatehouse (33 Chancery Lane). (www.lincolnsinn.org.uk)

Piccadilly Circus   SQUARE

10 ◉ MAP P74, C5

Architect John Nash had originally designed Regent St and Piccadilly in the 1820s to be the two most elegant streets in London but, restrained by city planners, he couldn't fully realise his dream. He may be disappointed, but suitably astonished, by Piccadilly Circus today: a traffic maelstrom, deluged by

visitors and flanked by high-tech advertisements.

St James's Piccadilly   CHURCH

11 ◉ MAP P74, B6

The only church (1684) Christopher Wren built from scratch and one of a handful established on a new site (most of the other London churches are replacements for those destroyed in the Great Fire), this simple building substitutes what some might call the pompous flourishes of Wren's most famous churches with a warm and elegant accessibility. The baptismal font portraying Adam and Eve and the altar reredos are by Grinling Gibbons. The church featured in the global hit Netflix series *Bridgerton*. (www.sjp.org.uk)

St Martin-in-the-Fields   CHURCH

12 ◉ MAP P75, E5

This parish church to the Royal Family is a delightful fusion of neoclassical and baroque styles. It was designed by architect James Gibbs, completed in 1726 and served as a model for many wooden churches in New England, USA. The church is well known for its excellent classical music concerts, many by candlelight (£9 to £32), and its links to the Chinese community (with services in English, Mandarin and Cantonese). (www.stmartin-in-the-fields.org)

All Saints Margaret Street

CHURCH

13 ⊙ MAP P74, A1

In 1859, architect William Butterfield completed one of the country's most supreme examples of High Victorian Gothic architecture, with extraordinary tiling and sumptuous stained glass. All Saints was selected by the head of English Heritage in 2014 as one of the top 10 buildings in the UK that have changed the face of the nation, a list that included Westminster Abbey and Christ Church in Oxford. (www.allsaints-margaretstreet.org.uk)

Eating

Spring

BRITISH £££

14 ✕ MAP P75, H4

White walls, ball chandeliers and columns are offset by the odd blossom in this restored Victorian drawing room in Somerset House (p76). Award-winning Australian chef Skye Gyngell leads a team dedicated to deliciousness and sustainability – no single-use plastic and an exclusive partnership with a biodynamic farm in Herefordshire to source its produce.

The early-evening scratch menu (£25 for three courses) uses food that would otherwise be wasted. (www.springrestaurant.co.uk)

The Barbary

MEDITERRANEAN ££

15 ✕ MAP P75, E3

Taking inspiration from the 16th century Barbary Coast (basically the Mediterranean), this tiny restaurant packs a punch with superb small plates of whole roasted cauliflower laced in a deeply spiced salsa, deconstructed hummus, harissa lamb chop and octopus in pomegranate molasses. The flatbread comes out billowing from the tandoor oven, while the 'Jerusalem bagel' will forever ruin shop-bought bagels for you.

Fourth Plinth Project

ⓘ

Three of the four plinths at the corners of Trafalgar Sq are occupied by notables: King George IV on horseback, and military men General Sir Charles Napier and Major General Sir Henry Havelock. The fourth, originally intended for a statue of William IV, remained largely vacant for more than a century and a half. The Royal Society of Arts conceived what is now called the Fourth Plinth Commission in 1999, deciding to use the empty space for works by contemporary artists. Works exhibited for 18 months in 'the smallest sculpture park in the world' are invariably both fun and challenging, creating a sense of dissonance with the grand surrounds of Trafalgar Sq.

St Giles-in-the-Fields, a Litany of Miseries

ⓘ

Built in what was used to be countryside between the City of London and Westminster, **St Giles-in-the-Fields** (www.stgilesonline.org) isn't much to look at but its history is a chronicle of London's most miserable inhabitants. The current structure (1733) is the third to stand on the site of an original chapel built in the 12th century to serve as a hospital for lepers.

Until 1547, when the hospital closed, prisoners on their way to be executed at the Tyburn Tree stopped at the church gate and sipped a large cup of soporific ale – their last refreshment – from St Giles's Bowl. From 1650, the prisoners were buried in the church grounds. It was also within the boundaries of St Giles that the Great Plague of 1665 took hold.

In Victorian times, it was London's worst slum, often mentioned in Dickens' novels. Today the drug users who hang out around the area make it feel like things haven't changed much.

An interesting relic in the church (northern side) is the plain white pulpit that was used for 40 years by John Wesley, the founder of Methodism.

The extensive and original drinks menu is another highlight, featuring excellent wines from Lebanon to Morocco and everywhere in between. (www.thebarbary.co.uk)

Berenjak

IRANIAN ££

16 🍴 MAP P74, D3

This Soho re-interpretation of Tehran's hole-in-the-wall kebab houses is a triumph: from the tiled decor, to the exquisitely charred meat and vegetables and *tanoor*-baked flat breads, Berenjak is authentic and heaven on a plate. The hummus, made of black chickpeas, tahini, walnuts and sumac, is the most unctuous, smoothest concoction you'll ever have. Booking is strongly advised.

The £15 weekday lunch menu (bread, *mazeh* and a kebab) is top value, and vegetarians have plenty of choice. (https://berenjak london.com)

Foyer & Reading Room at Claridge's

BRITISH £££

17 🍴 MAP P74, A3

Refreshing the better sort of West End shopper since 1856, the jaw-dropping Foyer and Reading Room at Claridge's, refulgent with Art-Deco mirrors and a Dale Chihuly glass sculpture, really is a memorable dining space. Refined food is served at all mealtimes, but many choose to nibble in best aristocratic fashion on the finger sandwiches and pastries of a classic afternoon tea. Smart attire is always required. Book well in advance. (www.claridges.co.uk)

Kiln THAI ££

18 MAP P74, B4

Crowned the UK's best restaurant in 2018, this tiny Thai grill cooks up a storm in its long, narrow kitchen, overseen by diners on their stools. The short menu rides the small-plates wave. The beef-neck curry is phenomenal, as are the claypot-baked glass noodles. Note that most dishes contain shellfish and pork. (www.kilnsoho.com)

Kanada-Ya RAMEN £

19 MAP P75, E2

In the debate over London's best ramen, we're still voting for this one. With no reservations taken, queues can get impressive outside this tiny and enormously popular canteen, where ramen cooked in *tonkotsu* (pork-bone broth) draws in diners from near and far. The noodles arrive at just the right temperature and hardness, steeped in a delectable broth and rich flavours. (www.kanada-ya.com)

J Sheekey SEAFOOD £££

20 MAP P75, E4

A jewel of the Covent Garden dining scene, this incredibly smart restaurant was opened by 1890s fishmonger Josef Sheekey on the

Seven Dials Market

permission of Lord Salisbury (who wanted somewhere to eat after the theatre). It has five elegant wood-panelled rooms in which to savour the riches of the sea, cooked simply but exquisitely. Sheekey's fish pie and the grand shellfish platters are signature dishes. (www.j-sheekey.co.uk)

Delaunay
EUROPEAN ££

21 🍴 MAP P75, H3

This immaculate spot channels the majesty of the grand cafes of Central Europe. Schnitzels, sausages and fish take pride of place on the menu, which is rounded out with Alsatian *tarte flambée* (thin-crust 'pizzas' with crème fraiche, onions and bacon lardons) and a rotating *Tagesteller* (dish of the day). The more relaxed **Delaunay Counter** (www.thedelaunay.com/counter) is next door. (www.thedelaunay.com)

Seven Dials Market
STREET FOOD £

22 🍴 MAP P75, F3

In a former banana warehouse (thus the banana motif) and reminiscent of New York's famous Chelsea Market, this two-storey indoor street-food collective delivers everything from vegan tacos at Club Mexicana to Japanese soul food at the tiny outpost of Brixton's Nanban. Sun streams through the glass skylights by day, live music gets the party vibe going at night. (www.sevendials market.com)

Barrafina
TAPAS ££

23 🍴 MAP P75, F5

With no reservations, you may need to get in line for an hour or so at this restaurant that produces some of the best tapas in town. Divine mouthfuls are served on each plate, from the prawns with roasted *piquillo* pepper to the Iberian pork ribs and chargrilled artichokes, so you may think it worth the wait. (www.barrafina.co.uk)

Drinking

Artesian
COCKTAIL BAR

24 🚇 MAP P74, A1

For a dose of West End glamour with a touch of Oriental elegance, the sumptuous (often crowded) bar at the Langham hits many marks. Its cocktails (from £20) have won multiple awards, and the bar itself has been acclaimed the world's best. Its name acknowledges the 360ft-deep well beneath the hotel and, metaphorically, the immaculately designed 'source of indulgence' to be found within. (www.artesian-bar.co.uk)

Lamb & Flag
PUB

25 🚇 MAP P75, F4

Perpetually busy, the pint-sized Lamb & Flag is full of charm and history: there's been a public house here since at least 1772, when it was known as the Cooper's Arms and infamous for staging bare-knuckle boxing

West End on the Cheap

London, the West End especially, can be an expensive destination, but there are plenty of ways to make your pennies last. Many of the top museums are free, so give them priority over the more commercial attractions. The West End is compact, so choose to walk, take the bus (it's cheaper than the Tube) or hire a **Santander Cycle** (📞0343 222 6666; www.tfl.gov. uk/modes/cycling/santander-cycles). Finally, go out early – bars in the West End often have a 'happy hour' with cheaper drinks, and many restaurants offer good-value 'pre-theatre' menus.

matches. Rain or shine, you'll have to elbow your way through the merry crowd drinking outside to get to the bar. (www.lamband flagcoventgarden.co.uk)

Le Magritte Bar COCKTAIL BAR

26 🚇 MAP P74, A2

Sip a bourbon or a classic cocktail in the 1920s Art-Deco ambience of this stylish bar at the hallmark Beaumont hotel. It's central, glam and like a private members' club, but far from stuffy. Only a few years old, Le Margritte Bar feels like it's been pouring drinks since the days of the flapper and the jazz age. (www. thebeaumont.com/dining/american-bar)

American Bar COCKTAIL BAR

27 🚇 MAP P75, H5

Home of the Lonely Street, Concrete Jungle and other house cocktails named after iconic songs collected in the 'Savoy Songbook,' the seriously dishy American Bar is a London icon, with soft blue furniture, gleaming Art-Deco lines and live piano jazz from 6.30pm nightly. Cocktails start at £20 and peak at a stupefying £5000 (for the Sazerac, containing cognac from 1858). (www.thesavoylondon. com/restaurant/american-bar)

French House PUB

28 🚇 MAP P74, D4

This legendary, twin-storied bohemian boozer has quite a history: it was the meeting place of the Free French Forces during WWII and de Gaulle is said to have drunk here often, while Dylan Thomas, Peter O'Toole and Francis Bacon all measured their length on the wooden floor at least once. Expect to share space with media and theatre types enjoying liquid lunches. (www.frenchhousesoho.com)

Heaven GAY

29 🚇 MAP P75, F6

Encouraging hedonism since 1979, when it opened on the site of a former roller disco, this perennially popular mixed/gay bar under the Charing Cross arches hosts excellent gigs and club nights, and has hosted New Order, Adele, Lady Gaga, Year &

Years and many a legendary act. Monday's mixed party Popcorn offers one of the best weeknight's clubbing in the capital. (www.heavennightclub-london.com)

Gordon's Wine Bar   WINE BAR

30 🚇 MAP P75, G6

Quite possibly the oldest wine bar in London (it opened in 1890), cavernous, candlelit and atmospheric Gordon's is a victim of its own success – it's relentlessly busy, and unless you arrive before the office crowd does, forget about landing a table. Nibble on cheese, bread and olives with your plonk – there's even a vegan/organic wine list. (https://gordonswinebar.com)

Entertainment

Ronnie Scott's   JAZZ

31 ⭐ MAP P74, D3

Ronnie Scott's jazz club opened in 1959 and became widely known as Britain's best, hosting such luminaries as Miles Davis, Charlie Parker, Ella Fitzgerald, Count Basie and Sarah Vaughan. The club continues to build upon its formidable reputation by presenting a range of big names and new talent. Book in advance, or come for a more informal gig at **Upstairs @ Ronnie's**. (www.ronniescotts.co.uk)

Royal Opera House   OPERA

32 ⭐ MAP P75, G3

Opera and ballet have a fantastic setting on Covent Garden Piazza,

Ronnie Scott's

Regent Street

The handsome border dividing bar-hoppers of Soho from the Gucci-heeled hedge-fund managers of Mayfair, Regent St was designed by John Nash as a ceremonial route linking Carlton House, the Prince Regent's long-demolished town residence, with the 'wilds' of Regent's Park. Nash had to downsize his plan and build the thoroughfare on a curve, but Regent St is today a well-subscribed shopping street lined with some lovely listed buildings.

Its anchor tenant is undoubtedly **Hamleys**, London's premier toy and game shop. Regent St is also famous for its **Christmas light displays**, which get switched on with some fanfare (usually around mid-November).

and a night here is a sumptuous affair. Although the programme has modern influences, the main attractions are still the classic productions with their world-class performers. A three-year, £50-million revamp finished in October 2018, with new areas open to the non-ticketed public for the first time, including the cafe and bar. (www.roh.org.uk)

Wigmore Hall CLASSICAL MUSIC

33 ⭐ MAP P74, A1

Wigmore Hall, built in 1901 as a piano showroom, is one of the best and most active classical-music venues in town, with more than 460 concerts a year. This isn't just because of its fantastic acoustics, beautiful Arts and Crafts–style cupola over the stage and great variety of concerts, but also because of the sheer quality of the performances. (www.wigmore-hall.org.uk)

Donmar Warehouse THEATRE

34 ⭐ MAP P75, E3

The 250-seat Donmar Warehouse is London's 'thinking person's theatre'. With artistic director Michael Longhurst, works in progress are more provocative and less celebrity-driven than traditional West End theatre. (www.donmarwarehouse.com)

Shopping

Foyles BOOKS

35 🔒 MAP P74, D3

London's most legendary bookshop, where you can find even the most obscure titles, is a joy to explore. There are extensive sections on virtually everything from children's books to cooking, history to music. The cafe is on the 5th floor, plus a small gallery for art exhibitions. Grant & Cutler, the UK's largest foreign-language bookseller, is on the 4th floor. (www.foyles.co.uk)

Stanfords
BOOKS

36 🔒 MAP P75, F3

Trading since 1853, this grand-daddy of travel bookshops and seasoned seller of maps, guides and globes is a destination in its own right. Polar explorer Ernest Shackleton, Victorian missionary David Livingstone and writer and presenter Michael Palin have all shopped here. In 2019 Stanfords left the iconic Long Acre building it had been housed in since 1901 and moved around the corner to this new address. (www.stanfords.co.uk)

Hamleys
TOYS

37 🔒 MAP P74, A4

The biggest and oldest toy emporium in the world, Hamleys houses six floors of fun for kids of all ages, from the basement's gaming and Harry Potter collections up to Lego World on the 5th floor. Staff on each level have opened the packaging and are playing with everything from boomerangs to bubbles. Kids will happily spend hours here planning their Santa letters. (www.hamleys.com)

Sounds of the Universe
MUSIC

38 🔒 MAP P74, C3

Outlet of the **Soul Jazz Records** label: explorers of wild, wonderful and often forgotten corners of black music who bring back gems for their legendary compilations. Vinyl fetishists will love the many brilliant, previously rare reissues on sale. (https://soundsoftheuniverse.com)

Neal's Yard Dairy
FOOD

39 🔒 MAP P75, F3

A fabulous, fragrant cheese house that would fit in somewhere in rural England, this place is proof that Britain can produce top-quality cheeses in most classes. There are more than 70 varieties of English and Irish cheeses that the shopkeepers will let you taste, including independent farmhouse brands. Condiments, pickles, jams and chutneys are also on sale. www.nealsyarddairy.co.uk)

Vivienne Westwood
FASHION & ACCESSORIES

40 🔒 MAP P74, A4

The fashion doyenne of the punk and new-wave aesthetic, Westwood has always had a reputation for being controversial and political. She continues to design collections as bold, innovative and provocative as ever, featuring 19th-century-inspired bustiers, wedge shoes, tartan and sharp tailoring. (www.viviennewestwood.com)

Liberty
DEPARTMENT STORE

41 🔒 MAP P74, A3

One of London's most recognisable shops, Liberty department store has a white-and-wood-beam Tudor Revival facade that lures shoppers in to browse luxury contemporary fashion, homewares, cosmetics and accessories, all at sky-high prices. A classic London gift or souvenir is a Liberty fabric print, especially in the form of a scarf. (www.libertylondon.com)

Explore ◈
British Museum & Bloomsbury

Bookish Bloomsbury puts a leisurely and genteel spin on central London. Home to the British Museum, the British Library, universities, publishing houses, literary pubs and gorgeous Georgian squares, Bloomsbury is deeply but accessibly cultured. You could spend all day in the British Museum, but there's a tantalising choice of options outside, with excellent pubs and restaurants nearby.

The Short List

○ *British Museum (p90)* Admiring ancient civilisations going back seven millennia.

○ *British Library (p98)* Learning about the treasures of the English language.

○ *Wellcome Collection (p98)* Exploring a unique museum where science and art meet.

○ *Coal Drops Yard (p98)* Strolling the newly redeveloped industrial heartland by Kings Cross.

○ *London Review Bookshop (p104)* Browsing a wide range of titles at this excellent bookshop.

Getting There & Around

Ⓤ Get off at Tottenham Court Rd (Northern and Central Lines), Goodge St (Northern Line), Russell Sq (Piccadilly Line) or Euston Sq (Circle, Hammersmith & City and Metropolitan Lines).

🚌 For the British Museum and Russell Sq, take bus 98 along Oxford St; bus 91 runs from Whitehall/Trafalgar Sq to the British Library and onto King's Cross.

British Museum & Bloomsbury Map on p96

British Library (p98) TK KURIKAWA/SHUTTERSTOCK ©

Top Experience 📷
Wander Through Time at the British Museum

Britain's most visited attraction for a decade, the British Museum draws in 5.8 million visitors each year. It's an exhilarating stampede through world cultures over millennia, with 90 galleries of over 80,000 exhibits devoted to ancient civilisations, from Egypt to western Asia, the Middle East, Rome and Greece, India, Africa, prehistoric and Roman Britain, and medieval antiquities.

◉ MAP P97, C7

www.britishmuseum.org

Great Russell St

admission free

🕐 10am-5pm (last entry 4pm)

Ⓤ Tottenham Court Rd or Russell Sq

History of the Museum

The museum was founded in 1753 when royal physician Hans Sloane sold his 'cabinet of curiosities' for the then-princely sum of £20,000, raised by national lottery. The collection opened to the public for free in 1759, and the museum has since kept expanding through judicious acquisitions, bequests and controversial imperial plundering.

The Great Court

The first thing you'll see on entry is the Great Court covered with a spectacular glass-and-steel roof designed by Norman Foster in 2000. It is the largest covered public square in Europe. In its centre is the celebrated **Reading Room**, currently closed, which has been frequented by the big brains of history, from Mahatma Gandhi to Karl Marx.

Enlightenment Galleries

Formerly known as the King's Library, this stunning neoclassical space (room 1) just off the Great Court was built between 1823 and 1827 and was the first part of the new museum building as it is seen today. Through fascinating artefacts, the collection traces how such disciplines as biology, archaeology, linguistics and geography emerged during the Enlightenment of the 18th century.

Ancient Egypt

The star of the show is the Ancient Egypt collection upstairs. It comprises sculptures, fine jewellery, papyrus texts, coffins and mummies, including the beautiful and intriguing **Mummy of Katebet** (room 63). The most prized item in the museum is the **Rosetta Stone** (room 4), the key to deciphering Egyptian hieroglyphics. Nearby is the enormous bust of the pharaoh **Ramesses II** (room 4).

★ **Top Tips**

o The museum has two entrances: one on Great Russell St and the other on Montague Pl (usually less busy).

o The museum offers activity backpacks for children (by age) to make their visit much more engaging. They also have explorer trails and art kits. Head to the Families Desk in the Great Hall for great advice and resources.

✕ **Take a Break**

The British Museum is vast so you'll need to recharge. Make sure you book lunch at Honey & Co (p100).

If it's a pint you're after, do as Karl Marx did and head to the Museum Tavern (p102) across the road.

Conquering the Museum

The museum is huge, so pick a gallery or theme for your visit to avoid being overwhelmed, or consider taking a tour. There are free 40-minute **Eye-Opener tours** of individual galleries (check the website or the information desk for time and details), and **Around the World in 90 Minutes tours** from Friday to Sunday (£14, limited capacity). Since the pandemic, audio guides have been replaced by an app (£4.99), which you can download ahead of your visit. It contains curated tours as well as expert commentary on 250 highlighted objects in five languages.

Assyrian Treasures

Assyrian treasures from ancient Mesopotamia include the **winged bulls** from Khorsabad (room 10), at 16 tonnes the heaviest object in the museum. Behind it are the exquisite **lion hunt reliefs** from Ninevah (room 10) dating from the 7th century BCE, which influenced Greek sculpture. Such antiquities are all the more significant after the so-called Islamic State's bulldozing of Nimrud in 2015.

Parthenon Sculptures

The controversial Parthenon sculptures (room 18) were taken from Athens' Acropolis by Lord Elgin (British ambassador to the Ottoman Empire) in 1801. The 80m-long marble frieze is thought to be of the Great Panathenaea, a festival in honour of the Greek goddess Athena held every four years.

Mildenhall Treasure & Lindow Man

Upstairs are finds from Britain and the rest of Europe (rooms 40 to 51). Many go back to Roman times, when the empire spread across much of the continent, including the Mildenhall Treasure (room 49), a collection of almost three dozen pieces of 4th-century-CE Roman silverware unearthed in Suffolk with both pagan and early Christian motifs. **Lindow Man** (room 50) is the well-preserved remains of a 1st-century man discovered in a bog near Manchester in northern England in 1984.

Sutton Hoo Ship Burial

The medieval artefacts from the Sutton Hoo Ship Burial (room 41), an elaborate Anglo-Saxon burial site from Suffolk dating from the 7th century, are another unmissable highlight of the museum.

Lewis Chessmen

Perennial favourites are the lovely Lewis Chessmen (room 40), some of the 82 12th-century game pieces carved from walrus tusk and whale teeth that were found on a remote Scottish island in the early 19th century.

British Museum

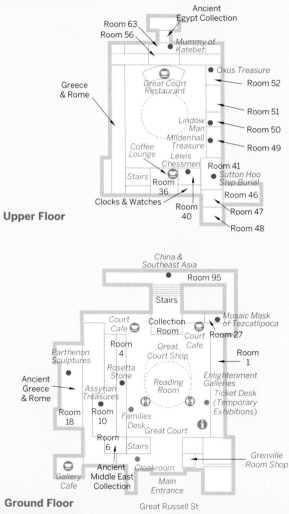

Upper Floor

Ancient Egypt Collection
Room 63
Room 56
Mummy of Katebet
Greece & Rome
Great Court Restaurant
Oxus Treasure
Room 52
Room 51
Lindow Man
Room 50
Mildenhall Treasure
Room 49
Coffee Lounge
Lewis Chessmen
Room 41
Sutton Hoo Ship Burial
Stairs
Room 36
Room 46
Clocks & Watches
Room 40
Room 47
Room 48

Ground Floor

China & Southeast Asia
Room 95
Stairs
Court Cafe
Room 4
Collection Room
Mosaic Mask of Tezcatlipoca
Court Cafe
Room 27
Parthenon Sculptures
Great Court Shop
Room 1
Rosetta Stone
Ancient Greece & Rome
Assyrian Treasures
Reading Room
Enlightenment Galleries
Ticket Desk (Temporary Exhibitions)
Room 18
Room 10
Families Desk
Room 6
Great Court
Stairs
Gallery Cafe
Ancient Middle East Collection
Cloakroom
Main Entrance
Grenville Room Shop
Great Russell St

Walking Tour 🥾

A Literary Walk Around Bloomsbury

Bloomsbury is indelibly associated with the literary figures that made this part of London their home. Charles Dickens, JM Barrie, WB Yeats, Virginia Woolf, TS Eliot, Sylvia Plath and other bold-faced names of English literature have all been associated with properties delightfully dotted around Bloomsbury and its attractive squares.

Walk Facts

Start Bedford Sq;
Ⓤ Goodge St

End Museum Tavern;
Ⓤ Holborn or Tottenham
Court Rd

Length 1.1 miles; two to
three hours

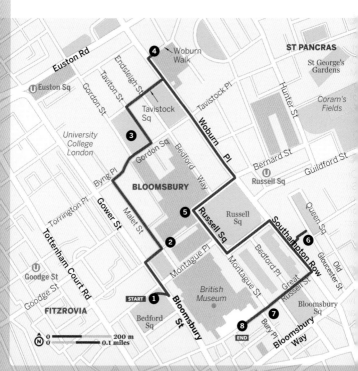

❶ Bedford Square

An eye-catching symbiosis of Bloomsbury's creative heritage and architectural charms, Bedford Sq is London's best-preserved Georgian square. The main office of Bloomsbury Publishing (which notably publishes the Harry Potter books) is at No 50. Sir Anthony Hope Hawkins, author of *The Prisoner of Zenda,* lived at No 41, while the Pre-Raphaelite Brotherhood was founded around the corner at 7 Gower St in 1848.

❷ Senate House

Along student-thronged Malet St, the splendid but intimidating Art-Deco Senate House served as the Ministry of Information in WWII, inspiring George Orwell's Ministry of Truth in his novel *Nineteen Eighty-Four.* Orwell's wife, Eileen, worked in the censorship department between 1939 and 1942.

❸ Gordon Square

Once a private square, Gordon Sq is open to the public and a lovely place for a rest. Locals sit on benches reading, chatting and eating sandwiches when the sun shines. Blue plaques attest to the presence of literary greats.

❹ Woburn Walk

Irish poet and playwright WB Yeats lived at 5 Woburn Walk, a genteel lane just south of the church of St Pancras. A leading figure of the Celtic Revival and author of *The Tower,* WB Yeats was born in Dublin, but spent many years in London.

❺ Faber & Faber

The former offices of Faber & Faber are at the northwest corner of Russell Sq, marked with a blue plaque about TS Eliot, the American poet and playwright and first editor at Faber. The gardens and fountain at the centre of Russell Sq are great for recuperation, preferably on a bench under the trees.

❻ St George the Martyr

The 18th-century church of St George the Martyr, across from the historic **Queen's Larder** (p102) pub at the south end of Queen Sq, was where Ted Hughes and Sylvia Plath were married on 16 June in 1956 (aka Bloomsday). They chose this date in honour of James Joyce.

❼ London Review Bookshop

It wouldn't be Bloomsbury without a good bookshop and the London Review Bookshop (p104) is one of London's finest. Affiliated with the *London Review of Books*, it has an eclectic selection of books and DVDs. Bookworms spend hours browsing the shelves or absorbed in new purchases in the shop's cafe.

❽ Museum Tavern

Karl Marx used to down a well-earned pint at the Museum Tavern (p102) after a hard day inventing communism in the British Museum Reading Room.

British Museum & Bloomsbury

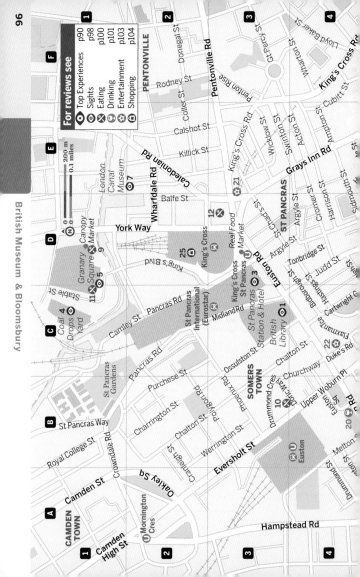

For reviews see

◉	Top Experiences	p90
◉	Sights	p98
✕	Eating	p100
◉	Drinking	p101
◉	Entertainment	p103
◉	Shopping	p104

PENTONVILLE

Donegal St

Rodney St

Collier St

Calshot St

Killick St

Pentonville Rd

Penton Rise

Gt Percy St

Wharton St

King's Cross Rd

Wicklow St

Swinton St

Acton St

Cubitt St

Amwell St

Lloyd Baker St

King's Cross Rd

Grays Inn Rd

Lloyd's Row

Caledonian Rd

Wharfdale Rd

Balfe St

London
Canal
Museum

◉7

York Way

12 ✕

ST PANCRAS

◉21

St Chad's St

Argyle St

Argyle Sq

Cromer St

Harrison St

Leigh St

0   200 m
0   0.1 miles

Granary
Square
Market

Stable St

11 ✕

◉5

◉9

Canopy
Market

Ⓝ

Coal
Drops
Yard

4

King's Blvd

King's Cross

25

Real Food
Market

King's Cross
St Pancras Ⓤ

Euston Rd

Tonbridge St

Judd St

Hastings St

Cartwright G

Camley St

Pancras Rd

St Pancras
International
(Eurostar)

Ⓐ

Midland Rd

King's Cross
St Pancras
Station & Hotel

3

◉1

British
Library

Bidborough St

22

Flaxmance

Pancras Rd

St Pancras
Gardens

Ossulston Rd

Chalton St

SOMERS
TOWN

Churchway

Duke's Rd

St Pancras Way

Purchese St

Charrington St

Chalton St

Polygon Rd

Phoenix Rd

Drummond Cres

Dick Way

10

Upper Woburn Pl

20 Ⓤ Rd

Royal College St

Crowndale Rd

Camden St

Cranleigh St

Werrington St

Eversholt St

Euston St

Ⓤ Euston

Melton St

Drummond St

CAMDEN
TOWN

Camden
High St

Ⓤ Mornington
Cres

Oakley Sq

Hampstead Rd

A   B   C   D   E   F

1   2   3   4

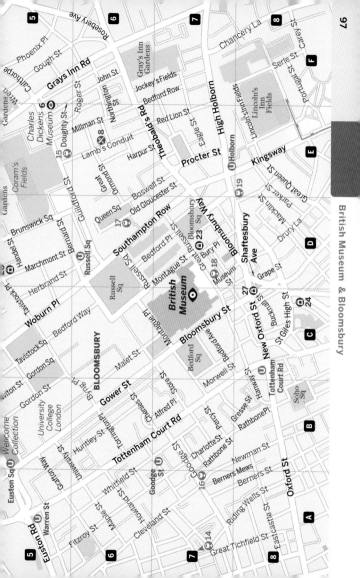

British Museum & Bloomsbury

5

Rosebery Ave

Phoenix Pl

Gough St

Wren

Calthorpe

Gardens

Grays Inn Rd

Charles
Dickens
Museum 6

Doughty St

Roger St

John St

Northington St

Millman St

15

8

Lamb's Conduit

Harpur St

Great Ormond St

Boswell St

Old Gloucester St

Queen Sq

17

Gray's Inn
Gardens

Jockey's Fields

Bedford Row

Red Lion St

Theobald's Rd

Proctor St

Southampton Row

Bedford Pl

Russell St

Montague St

Bloomsbury Way

23

Great Bury Pl

18

Museum St

Bloomsbury St

Bedford Ave

Bedford
Sq

Morwell St

British
Museum

High Holborn

Eagle St

Holborn

Kingsway

Procter St

Chancery La

Serle St

Portugal St

Carey

Lincoln's Inn Fields

Lincoln's
Inn
Fields

19

Great Queen St

Parker St

Macklin St

Drury La

Shaftesbury
Ave

Grape St

New Oxford St

27

St Giles High St

Buckingham St

24

Tottenham
Court Rd

Soho
Sq

Hanway St

Gresse St

Rathbone Pl

Charlotte St

Rathbone St

Newman St

Berners Mews

Berners St

Oxford St

Coram's
Fields

Gardens

Handel St

Brunswick Sq

Bernard St

Marchmont St

Herbrand St

Woburn Pl

Bedford Way

Russell
Sq

Russell Sq

BLOOMSBURY

Tavistock Sq

Gordon Sq

Malet St

Gower St

Byng Pl

Bedford Sq

Store St

Montague Pl

Euston Sq

Wellcome
Collection

University
College
London

Gordon St

Huntley St

Torrington Pl

Chenies St

Alfred Pl

Grafton Way

Eviton St

Keppel St

Tottenham Court Rd

Goodge St

13

Whitfield St

16

Goodge St

Percy St

Maple St

Howland St

Cleveland St

Euston Rd

Warren St

Fitzroy

14

Great Tichfield St

Riding Wells St

Eastcastle St

Sights

British Library

LIBRARY

1 ⊙ MAP P96, C3

Consisting of low-slung, red-brick terraces and fronted by a large piazza with an oversized statue of Sir Isaac Newton, Colin St John Wilson's British Library building is an architectural wonder. Completed in 1998, it's home to some of the greatest treasures of the written word, including the *Codex Sinaiticus* (the first complete text of the New Testament), Leonardo da Vinci's notebooks and two copies of the Magna Carta (1215). (www.bl.uks)

Wellcome Collection

MUSEUM

2 ⊙ MAP P97, B5

Under a new director Melanie Keen (appointed in 2019), Wellcome Collection committed to addressing the challenges of its less enlightened beginnings. The museum focuses on the interface of art, science and medicine. At its heart is Sir Henry Wellcome's collection of (at times controversial) medical curiosities (saws for amputation, forceps through the ages, sex aids and amulets). Beyond the permanent galleries, there are absorbing temporary exhibitions, plus a great cafe and a fantastic shop. (www.wellcomecollection.org)

St Pancras Station & Hotel

HISTORIC BUILDING

3 ⊙ MAP P96, D3

Looking at the jaw-dropping Gothic splendour of St Pancras (1868), it's hard to believe that the Midland Grand Hotel languished empty for decades and even faced demolition in the 1960s. Now home to a five-star hotel, 67 luxury apartments and the Eurostar terminal, the entire complex has regained its former glory. Tours (£25; 10.30am, noon, 2pm and 3.30pm Saturday and Sunday; book through the hotel) take you on a fascinating journey through the building's history, from its inception as the southern terminus for the Midland Railway line. (www.marriott.co.uk)

Coal Drops Yard

AREA

4 ⊙ MAP P96, C1

The latest part of post-industrial King's Cross to be regenerated is this double-level shopping and eating arcade, curving its way along the Regent's Canal, just west of Granary Sq. Beautifully restored buildings from the 1850s were used to transfer coal from rail wagons to road carts (and, later, for '80s raves). Now they're now home to independent clothing outlets, a range of restaurants and bars, and changing art installations (www.coaldropsyard.com)

Granary Square

SQUARE

5 ◉ MAP P96, D1

Positioned on a sharp bend in the Regent's Canal north of King's Cross Station, Granary Sq is at the heart of a major redevelopment of a 27-hectare expanse, once full of abandoned freight warehouses and an enormous granary. The square's most striking feature is the fountain made of 1080 individually lit water jets, which pulse and dance in sequence. On hot spring and summer days, it becomes a busy urban beach. (www.kingscross.co.uk)

Charles Dickens Museum

MUSEUM

6 ◉ MAP P97, E5

The prolific writer Charles Dickens lived with his growing family in this handsome four-storey Georgian terraced house for a mere 2½ years (1837–39), but this is where his work really flourished, as here he completed *The Pickwick Papers*, *Nicholas Nickleby* and *Oliver Twist*. Each of the dozen rooms, some restored to their original condition, which are wonderfully evocative of life in Victorian times, contains various memorabilia. You can download fun and informative audio guides directly on to your phone. (www.dickensmuseum.com)

Coal Drops Yard

Canal Mania 🛈

Approximately 4000 miles of canals were built in Britain between 1760 and 1830, a period known as 'Canal Mania', which heralded the Industrial Revolution. At the time the canals were the only practical way of transporting goods and materials.

The Regent's Canal also made a significant contribution to Victorian London: ice cream. Swiss entrepreneur Carlo Gatti used 'ice wells', two of which you can visit at the **London Canal Museum**, to store ice shipped from Norway. Gatti played a major part in developing cafe society by offering ice cream, coffee and waffles to the growing middle and working classes.

With the advent of rail in the 1830s, the canals entered a long period of decline. Today around 2000 miles remain, used mostly for recreation and environmental improvement.

By Brian Johnson, Volunteer at the London Canal Museum

London Canal Museum   MUSEUM

7 ◎ MAP P96, E2

This little museum on the Regent's Canal (p177) traces the history and everyday life of families living and working on London's impressively long and historic canal system. The exhibits in the stables upstairs are dedicated to the history of canal transport, including more recent developments such as the clean-up of the Lea River for the 2012 Olympic Games. The museum is housed in a warehouse dating from 1857, where ice was once stored in two deep wells. (www.canalmuseum.org.uk)

Eating

Honey & Co   MIDDLE EASTERN ££

8 ✖ MAP P97, E6

This culinary institution moved to its new location on the exquisite Lamb's Conduit St in 2022. The beautiful, airy and homey dining room is wonderful and the food – contemporary, delicious, seasonal Middle Eastern fare – has lost nothing of its flair. Expect plenty of perfectly executed sweet and savoury mixes such as peach salad with goat's cheese, and the best falafels this side of Jerusalem (https://honeyandco.co.uk/)

Ruby Violet   ICE CREAM £

9 ✖ MAP P96, D1

Ruby Violet takes ice cream to the next level: flavours are wonderfully original (masala chai, pink grapefruit and pineapple, banana caramel) and organic to boot (all sorbets are vegan too). Toppings and hot sauces are shop-made. Eat in or sit by the fountain on Granary Sq. (www.rubyviolet.co.uk)

Roti King   MALAYSIAN £

10 ⊗ MAP P96, B3

Roti King's pocket size and unwavering popularity mean queuing is inevitable, but we promise it will be worth the wait. It's all about roti canai (£6.50–£7.95), a flaky flatbread typical of Malaysia, served with fragrant bowls of curry or stuffed with tasty fillings. At last, a genuine budget option that isn't a sandwich or a salad. (www.rotiking.com)

Caravan   INTERNATIONAL ££

11 ⊗ MAP P96, C1

Housed in the lofty Granary Building, the King's Cross redevelopment's first tenant (2012) is a vast industrial-chic destination for tasty fusion bites from around the world. You can opt for several small plates to share tapas-style, or stick to main-sized dishes. The outdoor seating area on Granary Sq is especially popular on warm days, and cocktails are popular regardless of the weather. (www.caravanrestaurants.co.uk)

Bar Pepito   TAPAS £

12 ⊗ MAP P96, D3

This tiny, intimate Andalusian bodega specialises in sherry and tapas. Novices fear not: the staff are on hand to advise. They're also experts at food pairings (top-notch ham and cheese selections). To go the whole hog, try a tasting flight of selected sherries with snacks to match. (https://camino.uk.com/restaurant/bar-pepito)

North Sea Fish Restaurant   FISH & CHIPS ££

13 ⊗ MAP P96, D4

Since 1977, the North Sea has set out to cook fresh fish and potatoes – a simple ambition in which it succeeds admirably. Jumbo-sized plaice, halibut, sole and other fillets are delivered daily, deep-fried or grilled, and served with plenty of chips. Buy from the original takeaway counter or sit down in the fully-fledged restaurant. (http://northseafishrestaurant.co.uk)

Drinking

Purl   COCKTAIL BAR

14 ⊕ MAP P97, A7

Purl is a fabulous underground drinking den – decked out in overstuffed vintage furniture in intimate nooks, and adorned with antique wood, stripped bricks and mementos of glorious past epochs like the silent-film era. Foams, aromas, unlikely garnishes and bespoke glassware give cocktails old and new an air of discovery, while subdued lighting and conversation add to the mysterious air.

It's all seated, across a variety of rooms and alcoves, and booking

Lunch on the Cheap 🍽

King's Cross is home to two excellent food stall markets: they're a great budget option, but they're also ideal to soak in the atmospheric pedestrian area around Regent's Canal, Granary Square and Coal's Drop Yard. From Wednesday to Friday, pick up goodies at the **Real Food Market** (www.realfoodfestival.co.uk) on King's Cross station's esplanade. From Friday to Sunday, head to the **Canopy Market** (www.canopymarket.co.uk) off Granary Square. Sit on a bench along the canal or among the planters at Coal's Drop Yard.

several days ahead is recommended – aim for Friday if you like live jazz. (www.purl-london.com)

Lamb   PUB

15 🚇 MAP P97, E5

With a curved mahogany bar topped with etched-glass 'snob screens' (swivelling panels concealing genteel Victorian drinkers from bar staff and other workers) and walls hung with antique lithographs, the Lamb seems the Platonic ideal of a London pub. Enjoy your Young's bitter on the deep-green upholstered banquettes, or in the walled beer garden in fine weather. (www.thelamblondon.com)

London Cocktail Club   COCKTAIL BAR

16 🚇 MAP P97, A7

Pendant bar lights, bright clutter, graffitied walls and a raucous atmosphere give a New York vibe to this snug basement saloon just north of Oxford St. If you prefer to drink seated, arrive early or hire the private booth: it gets pretty packed. The cocktail menu is about the length of the Brooklyn Bridge, with plenty of house specials. (www.londoncocktailclub.co.uk/goodge-street)

Queen's Larder   PUB

17 🚇 MAP P97, D6

This cheery local favourite takes its name from Queen Charlotte, who previously stored food here for her husband George III, during his nearby treatment for insanity. Food is no longer the main draw here: rather it's the snug bar and the handful of outdoor tables under the geranium-laden hanging baskets. (www.queenslarder.co.uk)

Museum Tavern   PUB

18 🚇 MAP P97, D7

Inaugurated in 1723, this storied pub has refreshed scholars from the British Museum's Reading Room including Karl Marx, George Orwell, Sir Arthur Conan Doyle and JB Priestley. Handsomely adorned with original late-Victorian etched glass, lead lighting and woodwork, it's popular with academics, students and travellers alike. It also serves pub classics from pies and burgers to a Sunday roast.

Princess Louise
PUB

19 🚇 MAP P97, E8

The gorgeous ground-floor saloon of this Sam Smith's pub, dating from 1872, boasts pressed-tin ceilings, handsome tiling, etched mirrors and 'snob screens', and a stunning central horseshoe bar. The original Victorian wood partitions provide plenty of private nooks, and typical pub food is served from noon to 2.30pm Monday to Friday, and 6pm to 8.30pm Monday to Thursday (mains £8 to £14).

Euston Tap
BAR

20 🚇 MAP P96, B4

This specialist drinking spot inhabits a monumental stone structure on the approach to Euston station. Craft-beer devotees can choose between 15 cask ales, 28 keg beers and 150 brews by the bottle. Grab a seat on the pavement, take the tight spiral staircase upstairs or buy a bottle to take away. (www.eustontap.com)

Entertainment

Scala
LIVE MUSIC

21 🌟 MAP P96, E3

Opened in 1920 as a cutting-edge golden-age cinema, Scala slipped into porn-movie hell in the 1970s,

Museum Tavern

only to be reborn as a club and live-music venue in the early 2000s. It's one of the top places in London to catch an intimate gig and is a great dance space too, hosting a diverse range of club nights. (www.scala.co.uk)

The Place   DANCE

22 ⭐ MAP P96, C4

The birthplace of modern British dance is one of London's most exciting cultural venues, still concentrating on challenging and experimental choreography. Behind the late-Victorian terra-cotta facade you'll find a 300-seat theatre, an arty, creative cafe atmosphere and a dozen training studios. Tickets usually cost from £18. (www.theplace.org.uk)

Shopping

London Review Bookshop   BOOKS

23 🔒 MAP P97, D7

The flagship bookshop of the *London Review of Books* fortnightly

Surf & Rest

Although the books are all securely hidden away in the member's-only reading rooms, the British Library (p98) is a tranquil spot to rest and revive. There's free wi-fi throughout the building, good cafes and restaurant, plus special exhibitions to see.

literary journal doesn't put faith in towering piles of books and slabs on shelves, but offers a wide range of titles in a handful of copies only. It often hosts high-profile author talks, and there's a charming cake shop where you can leaf through your new purchases. (www.londonreviewbookshop.co.uk)

Forbidden Planet   COMICS

24 🔒 MAP P97, C8

Forbidden Planet is a trove of comics, sci-fi, horror and fantasy literature, as well as action figures and toys, spread over two floors. It's an absolute dream for anyone into manga comics, off-beat genre titles, and sci-fi and fantasy memorabilia. (https://forbiddenplanet.com)

Harry Potter Shop at Platform 9¾   GIFTS & SOUVENIRS

25 🔒 MAP P96, D2

Pottermania refuses to die down and Diagon Alley remains impossible to find, but if you have junior witches and wizards seeking a wand of their own, take the family directly to King's Cross Station. This little wood-panelled shop also stocks jumpers sporting the colours of Hogwarts' four houses (Gryffindor having pride of place) and assorted merchandise, including, of course, the books. (www.harrypottershop.co.uk)

London's Bewildering Postcodes

The 20 arrondissements in Paris spiral clockwise from the centre in a lovely, logical fashion. Not so London's postcodes. Look at a map and you may be thinking: why does SE23 border SE6?

When they were introduced in 1858, the postcodes were fairly clear, with all the compass points represented, along with an east and west central (EC and WC). But not long afterwards NE was merged with E and S with SE and SW, and the problems began. The real convolution came during WWI when a numbering system was introduced for inexperienced sorters (regular employees were off fighting in 'the war to end all wars'). No 1 was the centre of each zone, but other numbers related to the alphabetical order of the postal districts' names. Thus anything starting with a letter near the beginning of the alphabet, like Chingford in East London, would get a low number (E4), even though it was miles from the centre at Whitechapel (E1), while Poplar, which borders Whitechapel, got E14.

It wasn't designed to confuse regular punters, but it does.

Gay's the Word

BOOKS

26 🔒 MAP P97, D5

The UK's first specifically gay and lesbian bookshop, this London institution has been selling LGB-TIQ+ works since 1979. It has a superb selection and a genuine community spirit, bolstered by its regular events. (www.gaystheword.co.uk)

James Smith & Sons Umbrellas

FASHION & ACCESSORIES

27 🔒 MAP P97, C8

Nobody makes and stocks such elegant umbrellas (not to mention walking sticks and canes) as this place. It's been fighting the British weather from the same address since 1857, and hopefully will be here for years to come. Prices reflect the quality. The beautiful old-school signage is worth a photo stop alone. (www.james-smith.co.uk)

Explore 🧭
St Paul's &
City of London

London's historic core is a tale of two cities: packed with weekday office workers and eerily quiet at weekends. For most of its history, the entire city was enclosed between sturdy walls that were only dismantled in the 18th century. The current millennium has seen daring skyscrapers sprout around the Square Mile, but the essential sights have been standing for hundreds of years: St Paul's Cathedral and the Tower of London.

The Short List

○ **Tower of London (p112)** Stepping through a treasury of history, past the colourful Beefeaters, spectacular Crown Jewels, soothsaying ravens and armour fit for a very large king.

○ **St Paul's Cathedral (p108)** Walking in awed reverence below the mighty dome of London's most beloved building before climbing 528 steps to the top.

○ **Barbican (p118)** Exploring London's preeminent cultural centre.

○ **Sky Garden (p118)** Marvelling at London's ultra-modern architecture from the penthouse urban jungle.

Getting There & Around

Ⓤ The City is served by seven tube lines and the DLR.

🚆 Numerous bus routes pass through the City's main streets.

⚓ Thames Clippers operates boats from Tower Millennium Pier and Blackfriars Pier.

St Paul's & City of London Map on p116

St Paul's Cathedral (p108) MARK CHILVERS/LONELY PLANET ©

Top Experience 📷
Stand in Awe at St Paul's Cathedral

Sir Christopher Wren's gleaming grey-domed masterpiece is the City of London's most magnificent building. Built between 1675 and 1710 after the Great Fire destroyed its predecessor, St Paul's was the first triple-domed cathedral in the world. Its vast, climbable cupolas still soar triumphantly over Ludgate Hill, offering sublime London panoramas, and some of the country's most celebrated citizens are interred in its crypt.

◎ MAP P116, D4

📞 020-7246 8357

www.stpauls.co.uk

St Paul's Churchyard

adult/child £17/7.20

🕘 8.30am-4pm Mon-Sat

Ⓤ St Paul's

Dome

Wren wanted to construct a dome that was imposing on the outside but not disproportionately large on the inside. The solution was to build it in three parts: a plastered brick inner dome, a nonstructural lead outer dome and a brick cone between them holding it all together, one inside the other. This unique structure, inspired by St Peter's Basilica in the Vatican, made the cathedral Wren's tour de force. Climb up the 528 stairs, thankfully in three stages, to access the cathedral's galleries.

Whispering Gallery

One would once enter through the door on the western side of the southern transept, where 257 steps lead to the interior walkway around the dome's base, 30m above the floor. However, for a number of years now the famous Whispering Gallery has been closed to the public with no immediate plans to reopen it.

Stone Gallery & Golden Gallery

Climbing another 119 steps brings you to the Stone Gallery, an outdoor viewing platform 53m above the ground, obscured by pillars and other safety measures. The remaining 152 iron steps to the Golden Gallery are steeper and narrower than below, but are worth the effort. From here, 85m above London, you can enjoy superb 360-degree views of the city.

Interior

At a time of anti-Catholic fervour, it was controversial to build a Roman-style basilica rather than using the more familiar Gothic style. St Paul's interiors were more reflective of Protestant tastes, being relatively unadorned, with large clear windows. The statues and mosaics seen today were added later.

★ Top Tips

o There's no charge to attend a service, but not all areas of the cathedral are accessible. To hear the cathedral choir, go to the 11.30am Sunday Eucharist or evensong (5pm Monday to Saturday and 3pm Sunday).

o Multimedia guides are included in the price of admission.

o Free guided tours depart several times a day (between 11am and 3pm); reserve a place at the tour desk, just past the entrance.

✗ Take a Break

Ivy Asia (p122) dishes up OTT fusion plates with views of the cathedral through its floor-to-ceiling windows. Cheaper British chain restaurants can be found in the streets nearby and the One New Change (p124) shopping centre.

Duke of Wellington Memorial

In the north aisle of the vast nave, you'll find the grandiose Duke of Wellington Memorial (1912), which took 54 years to complete. The Iron Duke's horse Copenhagen originally faced the other way, but it was deemed unfitting that a horse's rear end should face the altar. In contrast, beneath the dome is an elegant epitaph written for Wren by his son: *Lector, si monumentum requiris, circumspice* (Reader, if you seek his monument, look around you).

The Light of the World & the Quire

In the north transept chapel is William Holman Hunt's celebrated painting *The Light of the World* (1851–53), which depicts Christ knocking at a vine-covered door that, symbolically, can only be opened from within. In the heart of the cathedral, you'll find the spectacular quire (or chancel) – its ceilings and arches dazzling with colourful mosaics – and the **high altar**. The ornately carved choir stalls by Dutch-British sculptor Grinling Gibbons on either side of the quire are exquisite, as are the ornamental wrought-iron gates, separating the aisles from the altar, by French Huguenot Jean Tijou.

American Memorial Chapel

Walk around the altar, with its massive gilded oak **baldacchino** (canopy) with barley-twist columns, to the American Memorial Chapel, commemorating the 28,000 Americans based in Britain who lost their lives during WWII.

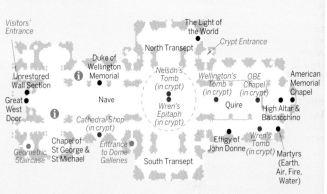

St Paul's Cathedral

Visitors' Entrance

The Light of the World

North Transept

Crypt Entrance

Unrestored Wall Section

Duke of Wellington Memorial

Nelson's Tomb (in crypt)

Wellington's Tomb (in crypt)

OBE Chapel (in crypt)

American Memorial Chapel

Great West Door

Nave

Wren's Epitaph (in crypt)

Quire

High Altar & Baldacchino

Cathedral Shop (in crypt)

Chapel of St George & St Michael

Entrance to Dome Galleries

South Transept

Effigy of John Donne

Wren's Tomb (in crypt)

Geometric Staircase

Martyrs (Earth, Air, Fire, Water)

Cathedral Floor & Crypt

Crypt

On the eastern side of the north transept, stairs lead down to the crypt and the **OBE Chapel**, where services are held for members of the Order of the British Empire. The crypt has memorials to around 300 of Britain's great and good, including Florence Nightingale, TE Lawrence (better known as Lawrence of Arabia) and Winston Churchill. Those actually buried here include the Duke of Wellington, Vice Admiral Horatio Nelson, Christopher Wren and the painters Joshua Reynolds, John Everett Millais, JMW Turner and William Holman Hunt. Also in the crypt are the cathedral's gift shop and toilets.

Churchyard & Surrounds

A **statue of Queen Anne** (the reigning monarch when St Paul's was built) stands at the cathedral steps, her gilded crown, sceptre and orb glinting in the sun. The figures at her feet represent Britannia, North America, France and Ireland. Made by sculptor Louis Auguste Malempré in 1886, it's a replica of the Francis Bird original from 1712.

Outside the north transept, the simple, squat and round **People of London Memorial**, honours the 32,000 civilians killed (and 50,000 seriously injured) during WWII.

Fifth Time Lucky

London's mother church has stood on this site since 604 CE. Wren's cathedral is the fifth incarnation, built to replace the soaring Gothic-style Old St Paul's after it was destroyed in the Great Fire in 1666. Old St Paul's was both longer and taller than Wren's version.

Tours Behind the Scenes

Multimedia guides are included in the price of a ticket, but it's worth signing up for the two tour options of St Paul's to get access to usually off-limits areas. Free **guided tours** cover most of the same ground as the audio guide, with the added bonus of being able to enter the quire for a better look at the ceiling mosaics. Check in at the tour desk as soon as you arrive. The **Triforium Tour** (£10) runs less frequently but includes the chance to descend the Geometric Staircase (the Divination Stairwell from the Harry Potter films), take in the BBC-exclusive view of the nave that's usually reserved for camera crews, see Wren's original oak model of St Paul's and visit the astounding library (reopening in 2023 after renovations).

Top Experience 📷
See the Crown Jewels at the Tower of London

With a history as bloody as it is fascinating, the Tower is London's most absorbing sight. Begun during the 11th-century reign of William the Conqueror, this royal fortress is in fact a castle containing 22 towers, and has served as a palace, observatory, armoury, mint, zoo, prison and execution site.

🎯 MAP P117, H5

www.hrp.org.uk/tower-of-london

Petty Wales

adult/child £25/12.50

🕓 9am-5.30pm, from 10am Sun & Mon

Ⓤ Tower Hill

Tower Green & Scaffold Site

What looks at first glance like a peaceful, almost village-like slice of the Tower's inner ward is actually one of its bloodiest. Those who have met their fate at the Scaffold Site include two of Henry VIII's wives, Anne Boleyn and Catherine Howard; 16-year-old Lady Jane Grey, who fell foul of Henry's daughter Mary I after her family attempted to have her crowned queen; and Robert Devereux, Earl of Essex, once a favourite of Elizabeth I. Just west of the scaffold site is **Beauchamp Tower** (1280), where high-ranking prisoners left behind unhappy inscriptions and other graffiti.

Chapel Royal of St Peter ad Vincula

On the northern edge of Tower Green is the 16th-century Chapel Royal of St Peter ad Vincula (St Peter in Chains), a rare surviving example of ecclesiastical Tudor architecture. Those buried here include three queens (Anne Boleyn, Catherine Howard and Lady Jane Grey) and two saints (Thomas More and John Fisher). A third saint, Philip Howard, was also interred here before his body was moved to Arundel in southern England.

Crown Jewels

To the east of the Chapel Royal and north of the White Tower is **Waterloo Barracks**, home of the Crown Jewels, which are in a very real sense priceless. The queue to get in can be long, but once inside, you'll be dazzled by lavishly bejewelled sceptres, orbs and crowns. Two moving walkways take you past crowns and other coronation regalia, including the platinum crown of the late Queen Mother, Elizabeth, which is set with the 106-carat Koh i-Nûr (Persian for 'Mountain of Light') diamond, and the Sovereign's Sceptre with Cross topped with the drop-shaped 530-carat Great Star of Africa diamond (also known as Cullinan I).

★ Top Tips

o Don't feel obliged to pay the additional Gift Aid price (which allows UK citizens to pass on a tax break to the Tower) on top of what is already a hefty admission fee.

o Purchase your ticket online for a 30-minute arrival slot.

o Start with a free Yeoman Warder tour, which is a great way to familiarise yourself with the site.

o Don't leave your visit too late in the day; ideally set aside three to four hours to see everything.

✕ Take a Break

Within the Tower walls, the **New Armouries Cafe** serves British standards in self-serve cafeteria-style setting. To the east at **St Katherine's Dock** there are a handful of cafes, restaurants and pubs to grab a bite to eat.

A bit further on, exhibited on its own, is the centrepiece: the Imperial State Crown, set with 2868 diamonds (including the 317-carat Second Star of Africa, also known as Cullinan II), sapphires, emeralds, rubies and pearls. It's worn by the monarch at the State Opening of Parliament.

White Tower

At the heart of the site is the oldest building left standing in the whole of London. Constructed from stone as a fortress in the 1070s, the White Tower was the original Tower of London – its current name arose after Henry III whitewashed it in the 13th century. Standing just 27m high, it's not exactly a skyscraper by modern standards, but in the Middle Ages it would have dwarfed the wooden huts surrounding the castle walls and intimidated the peasantry.

Most of its interior houses the **Royal Armouries** collection of cannons, guns, suits of chain mail, and armour for men and horses. One of the most remarkable exhibits in the Line of Kings are Henry VIII's suits of armour, including one made for him when he was a dashing 24-year-old and another when he was a bloated 50-year-old with a 129cm waist.

Chapel of St John the Evangelist

This unadorned 11th-century chapel, with its vaulted ceiling, rounded archways and 14 stone pillars, is a fine example of Norman architecture.

Bloody Tower

Bloody Tower (1225) takes its nickname from the princes in the Tower – 12-year-old Edward V and his younger brother, Richard – who were held here by their uncle and later thought to have been murdered to annul their claims to the throne. The blame is usually laid (notably by Shakespeare) at the feet of their uncle, Richard III. A small exhibition re-creates the study of explorer Sir Walter Raleigh – a repeat prisoner here – and looks at torture at the Tower, with gruesome replica devices like the Rack and the Scavenger's Daughter.

Medieval Palace

Inside **St Thomas's Tower** (built 1275–79) is a reconstructed hall and bedchamber from the time of Edward I. Adjoining **Wakefield Tower** (1220–40) was built by Edward's father, Henry III. It has been furnished with a replica throne and other decor.

Wall Walk

The huge inner wall of the Tower was added by Henry III from 1220 to improve the castle's defences. The Wall Walk allows you to tour its eastern and northern edge and the towers that punctuate it. Start at the **Salt Tower** and continue through the **Broad Arrow Tower** and **Constable Tower**, containing small displays on weapons and the Peasants' Revolt. The **Martin Tower**, which housed the Crown Jewels from 1669 to 1841, contains an exhibition about the original coronation regalia with

Tower of London Traditions

Yeomen Warders

The iconic Yeomen Warders, dressed in their signature red-trimmed navy uniform, have been guarding the Tower of London since the 15th century. Though their roles today are mostly ceremonial, they must have served at least 22 years in the British Armed Forces to qualify for the job. The Yeomen Warders are better known as the Beefeaters, a nickname that's been around since at least the 17th century. Its origins are unknown, although it's thought to be because of the large rations of beef – then a luxury – once given to them as part of their salary. But another tradition still lives on: Warders receive a bottle of Beefeater Gin on their birthday as part of an old arrangement with its producers for use of their image on the bottle.

Ravens

Superstition has it that if the Tower of London's six resident ravens ever leave, then the kingdom will fall. Call it silly, but the 350-year-old rumour is thought to have persisted since the reign of Charles II – who lived through the plague, the Great Fire and the execution of his father – and the Tower's guardians today still aren't taking any chances. The six required birds, plus one spare, are kept in an on-site aviary and are dutifully cared for by the in-house ravenmaster.

Ceremony of the Keys

Said to be the oldest military ceremony in the world, the elaborate locking of the Tower's main gates has been performed nightly without fail for more than 700 years. The Ceremony of the Keys begins precisely at 9.53pm, and it's all over by 10.05pm. Even when a bomb hit the Tower of London during the Blitz, the ceremony was delayed by only 30 minutes. Tickets to the Ceremony of the Keys cost £5 but must be booked online well in advance as they sell out quickly.

some of the older crowns on show (their precious stones removed).

Along the north wall, the **Brick Tower** has a fascinating display on the royal menagerie, including stories of a tethered polar bear that swam and fished in the Thames. The **Bowyer Tower** has exhibits about the Duke of Wellington, while the **Flint Tower** is devoted to the castle's role during WWI.

Tours

While officially guarding the Tower, the Yeomen Warders' main role is as tour guides. Entertaining 45-minute-long tours leave from the bridge near the main entrance every 30 minutes until 3.30pm (2.30pm in winter). Make this your first stop before exploring the Tower; it's included in the price of your ticket.

1

2

Farringdon Rd

Rosebery Ave

Clerkenwell Rd

Grays Inn Rd

Hatton Garden

Leather La

Greville St

Farringdon ⓤ

Cowcross St

HOLBORN

Chancery La ⓤ

High Holborn

New Fetter La

St Andrew St

Fetter La

Chancery La

Carey St

Fleet St

Strand

Essex St

Arundel St

Middle Temple La

Bouverie St

Whitefriars St

Salisbury Ct

Tudor St

New Bridge St

St Bride St

Victoria Embankment

Temple ⓤ

Inner
Temple
Gardens

Blackfriars ⓤ

Aylesbury St

Sekforde St

St John St

Britton St

St John's La

Turnmill St

Charterhouse St

West Smithfield

Farringdon St

Holborn
Viaduct

Old Bailey

Ludgate Hill

City
Thameslink

Puddle
Dock

White Lion Hill

Goswell Rd

Goswell Rd

Barbican ⓤ

Smithfield
Market

Long La

Aldersgate St

Golden Boy
of Pye Corner

Snow
Hill

Giltspur St

Newgate St

Angel
St

St Paul's ⓤ

St Paul's
Cathedral ⓞ

St Paul's Churchyard

One New
Change

Cannon

Queen Victoria St

Upper Thames

Blackfriars
Pier

Millennium
Bridge

Blackfriars
Bridge

Bankside
Pier

Bankside

SOUTH BANK

Park St

Blackfriars Rd

Southwark St

Southwark

Central St

Old St

Fann St

Golden La

Beech

Barbi

London

Foster La

Gresh

Cheaps

St
Alder

Southw
Bri

Goswell Rd

⊗ 8

14

⊙ 16

22 🛍

21 🛍

⊗ 13

For reviews see

ⓞ	Top Experiences	p108
⊙	Sights	p118
⊗	Eating	p121
🍷	Drinking	p122
✪	Entertainment	p124
🛍	Shopping	p124

Ⓝ

0 _____ 500 m
0 _____ 0.25 miles

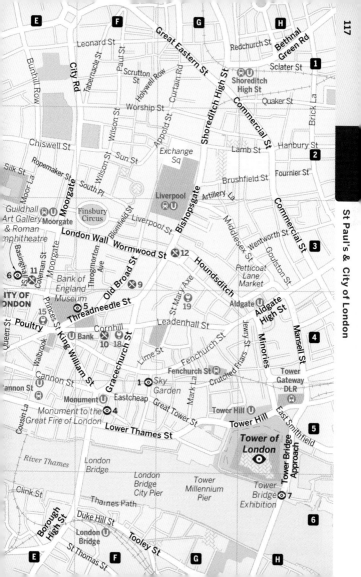

Sights

Sky Garden

VIEWPOINT

1 🔘 MAP P117, F5

The ferns, fig trees and purple African lilies that clamber up the final three storeys of the 'Walkie Talkie' skyscraper are mere wallflowers at this 155m-high rooftop garden – it's the extraordinary 360-degree views of London that make this vast, airport-terminal-like space so popular. The Sky Garden has front-row seats overlooking the Shard (p137) and vistas that gallop for miles east and west. Visits must be booked online in advance, and tickets run out quickly. (https://skygarden.london)

Barbican

St Mary Aldermary

CHURCH

2 🔘 MAP P116, D4

A Christoper Wren reconstruction, the church of St Mary Aldermary (1682) is unusual for the architect: it was built in Gothic style, and it's the only surviving church in the City of London of this type. Be prepared to spend some time gawping at the ceiling of the columned nave, covered in gleaming white plaster fan vaulting that's offset by the polished wood pews and medieval-style blood-red floor tiles. **Host Café** livens up the scene from its espresso bar and co-working space in the apse.

Barbican

ARCHITECTURE

3 🔘 MAP P116, D2

The architectural value of this sprawling post-WWII brutalist housing estate divides Londoners, but the Barbican remains a sought-after living space as well as the City's preeminent cultural centre. Public spaces include a quirky **conservatory** and the Barbican Centre (p124 theatres, cinema and two art galleries: **Barbican Art Gallery** and the **Curve**. Navigating the Barbican, designed to be a car-free urban neighbourhood, requires reliance on a network of elevated paths that didn't quite come to fruition. Find your bearings on an **architecture tour**. (www.barbican.org.uk)

JO CHAMBERS/SHUTTERSTOCK © ARCHITECT CHAMBERLIN, POWELL & BON ©

Sky Garden

Monument to the
Great Fire of London MONUMENT

4 ⊙ MAP P117, F5

Designed by Christopher Wren, this immense Doric column of Portland stone is a reminder of the Great Fire of London in 1666, which destroyed 80% of the city. It stands 62m high, the distance from the bakery in Pudding Lane where the fire is thought to have started. Although Lilliputian by today's standards, the Monument towered over London when it was built. Climbing up the column's 311 spiral steps still provides great views thanks to its central location. (www.themonument.org.uk)

Bank of
England Museum MUSEUM

5 ⊙ MAP P117, F4

This surprisingly interesting museum explores the evolution of money and the history of the Bank of England, founded in 1694, including its relationship with the transatlantic slave trade. Its centrepiece is a reconstruction of architect John Soane's original Bank Stock Office. Don't miss the chance to get your hands on a hefty 13kg solid-gold bar, worth more than £570,000. (www.bankofengland.co.uk/museum)

The Great Fire of London

London had for centuries been prone to fire, as nearly all buildings were constructed from wood and roofed with thatch, but the mother of all blazes broke out on 2 September 1666 in a bakery in Pudding Lane close to London Bridge. It didn't seem like much to begin with – the mayor himself dismissed it as something 'a woman might piss out' before going back to bed – but the unusual autumn heat combined with rising winds meant the fire raged out of control for four days, reducing 80% of London to ash. Only eight people died (officially at least), but most of medieval London was obliterated. The fire finally stopped at Pye Corner in Smithfield, then on the very edge of London, not before destroying 89 churches, including St Paul's Cathedral, and more than 13,000 houses, leaving tens of thousands of people homeless. The **Monument to the Great Fire of London** (p119) stands near the fire's start, and the small statue of a podgy naked **Golden Boy of Pye Corner, on the corner of** Cock Lane and Giltspur Street, marks the point where it burnt out.

Guildhall Art Gallery & Roman Amphitheatre GALLERY

6 ◉ MAP P117, E3

The City of London has had centuries to acquire an impressive art collection, which it's shown off since 1885. The original gallery was destroyed in the Blitz, and when the site was redeveloped in 1985, the remains of a Roman amphitheatre (c 70 CE) were discovered, so the gallery was redesigned to incorporate the ruins. The 4500-piece collection is particularly strong on London scenes and Victorian art, including significant pre-Raphaelite works by John Everett Millais and Dante Gabriel Rossetti. (www.cityoflondon.gov.uk/guildhallgalleries)

Tower Bridge Exhibition MUSEUM

7 ◉ MAP P117, H6

The inner workings of Tower Bridge can't compare with its exterior magnificence, but this geeky exhibition tries to bridge that gap with details of the construction and access to the Victorian steam-powered machinery that once raised the bascules. Archive footage at the start of the exhibition shows the bridge lifting for the first time, and girders in the South Tower show the bridge's original drab chocolate-brown paint job. Walking on the **glass floors** 42m above the River Thames is a highlight. (www.towerbridge.org.uk)

Eating

St. JOHN
BRITISH ££

8 ⊗ MAP P116, C2

As a pioneer of the nose-to-tail food movement in the UK, St. JOHN is likely to offer you offal and unusual cuts from a changing menu. Set in a former bacon smokehouse near Smithfield Market, with white-washed brick walls, high ceilings and simple wooden furniture, it's surely one of the most humble Michelin-starred restaurants anywhere. (www.stjohnrestaurant.com)

City Social
BRITISH £££

9 ⊗ MAP P117, F3

City Social pairs sublime sky-scraper views from its 24th-floor digs with delicate Michelin-starred cuisine. The interior is all Art-Deco inspired low-lit glamour. If you don't want to splash out on the full menu, opt for the bar, **Social 24**, which has longer hours and a compelling menu of nibbles (don't miss the goat's-cheese churros with locally sourced truffle-infused honey). (www.citysociallondon.com)

Simpsons Tavern
BRITISH £

10 ⊗ MAP P117, F4

'Old school' doesn't even come close to describing Simpsons, a City institution since 1757 and once frequented by Charles Dickens. Huge portions of traditional British grub are served to diners in dark-wood and olive-green booths. Save space for the

Simpsons Tavern

tavern's famous stewed-cheese dessert. (www.simpsonstavern.co.uk)

Hawksmoor Guildhall
STEAK ££

11 MAP P117, E3

Parquet floors, maroon leather seating and rich wood panelling create a cosy atmosphere in this subterranean steakhouse, one of a handful in a London-founded global chain. There's a decent-value set menu (2/3 courses £24/28) for lunch and early dinner. The Sunday roast is also a good option (noon to 4pm). Other British classics include chicken and fish. (https://thehawksmoor.com)

Duck & Waffle
BRITISH ££

12 MAP P117, G3

Duck and Waffle is a great spot for a late-night feed, open 24 hours over the weekend. Survey the kingdom from the highest restaurant in town (on the 40th floor) over a helping of the namesake dish: a fluffy waffle topped with a crispy leg of duck confit and a fried duck egg, drenched in mustard-seed maple syrup. (www.duckandwaffle.com)

Ivy Asia
ASIAN £££

13 MAP P116, D4

Ivy brings some late-night life into this part of the City with a nightly resident DJ, an extensive range of Japanese whiskies and OTT menu items like black-truffle dumplings that come sprinkled in gold leaf. The glowing green floor is made from semiprecious stones, and St Paul's Cathedral gleams through the windows. Also does a gorgeous Asian-inspired afternoon tea. (www.theivyasia.com)

Drinking

Oriole
COCKTAIL BAR

14 MAP P116, C3

Down a darkened alley through the eerie evening quiet of Smithfield Market is an unlikely spot for one of London's best cocktail bars, but the journey of discovery is the theme at speakeasy-style Oriole. The cocktail menu, divided into Old World, New World and the Orient, traverses the globe, with out-of-this-world ingredients including clarified octopus milk, strawberry tree curd and slow-cooked chai palm. (www.oriolebar.com)

Free View

Designed by French architect Jean Nouvel, **One New Change** (www.onenewchange.com) is a shopping centre housing mainly high-street brands, but take the lift to the 6th floor and a free open roof terrace will reward you with up-close views of the dome of St Paul's Cathedral and out over London.

City
Top Spots

Meals with a view Every London skyscraper now seems to come affixed with a high-altitude bar or restaurant. Get a taste of the high life at **City Social** (p121) or **Duck & Waffle**.

Classic boozers Though they tend to keep bankers' hours, the City's old-school restaurants and pubs are some of the most atmospheric and historic in town. **Viaduct Tavern**, a former Victorian gin palace, is one of the best.

Culture hub The City isn't London's cultural core, but the **Barbican Centre** (p118 & p124) is a powerhouse of innovative theatre, music and art.

Nickel Bar
COCKTAIL BAR

15 ⬚ MAP P117, E4

There's something *Great Gatsby*–ish about the Ned hotel: the elevated jazz pianists, the vast verdite columns, the classy American-inspired cocktails. Of all the public bars inside this magnificent former banking hall, the Nickel Bar soaks up the atmosphere best. Inspired by the glamorous Art-Deco saloons and the ocean-liner-era elegance, this is timeless nightcap territory. (www.thened.com/restaurants/the-nickel-bar)

Viaduct Tavern
PUB

16 ⬚ MAP P116, C3

Opened in 1869, the Viaduct Tavern is one of the only remaining Victorian gin palaces in the City, with etched-glass panes, blood-red embossed vines crawling along the ceiling, and even the old cashier's booth where drink tokens were purchased (because the bar staff weren't trusted with cash). The

tavern still specialises in gin, and a selection of house-made infusions beckons from behind the bar. (www.viaducttavern.co.uk)

Merchant House
COCKTAIL BAR

17 ⬚ MAP P117, E4

This well-hidden bar, on a feemingly forgotten alleyway off pedestrian-only Bow Lane, has some 600 whiskies, 400 rums and 400 gins. Don't worry about a novel-size drink list, the master mixologists will whip up a custom concoction based on your alcohol of choice and one of five taste palettes, including umami, tropical, coastal or smoke. (https://merchanthouse.bar)

Counting House
PUB

18 ⬚ MAP P117, F4

With its grand wooden staircase and painted ceilings edged with gold-coloured crown moulding, this pub, part of the Fuller's chain,

Getting into Nature in London

Springfield Park, in the north London neighbourhood of Stamford Hill, is a peaceful well-kept park with stunning views. It's an extension of the famous **Walthamstow Reservoir**, one of the largest urban wetlands in Europe. Next door, **Hackney Marshes** is the largest common land in Greater London. Not only is this area incredible for walks and wildlife, but there's also a great traditional pub tucked away on the bank of the canal. It's the perfect place to sit and watch the sunset with the locals.

By Ollie Olanipekun, Flock Together co-founder, @ollie_ranger / @flocktogether.world

is still every bit as dignified as when it opened as Prescott's Bank in 1893. Suited City folk crowd around the elegantly curved central bar under the domed skylight for the range of traditional cask ales and speciality pies. (www.the-counting-house.com)

Searcys at the Gherkin   BAR

19 🚇 MAP P117, G4

The top two floors of the iconic Gherkin skyscraper were once reserved as a private members' club, but now anyone dressed to impress is invited up. Cocktails in the 40th-floor **Iris** bar under the oculus roof with 360-degree views of the City are a sight to behold. On Sundays, **Helix**, the restaurant on the 39th floor, is open for a sky-high brunch. (https://searcysatthegherkin.co.uk)

Entertainment

Barbican Centre   PERFORMING ARTS

20 ⭐ MAP P116, D2

You'll get as lost in the astounding programme as you will in the labyrinthine brutalist building. Home to the **London Symphony Orchestra**, the **BBC Symphony Orchestra** and the **Royal Shakespeare Company**, the Barbican Centre is the City's premier cultural venue. It hosts concerts, theatre and dance performances, and screens indie films and Hollywood blockbusters at the cinema on Beech St. (www.barbican.org.uk)

Shopping

St Paul's Cathedral Shop   GIFTS & SOUVENIRS

21 🔒 MAP P116, C4

The place to come for essentials such as St Paul's tote bags and silk scarves printed with Cathedral artworks, the crypt shop also sells

London Silver Vaults

all of the usual Paddington Bear and double-decker bus souvenirs. (www.stpaulsshop.org.uk)

London Silver Vaults
ANTIQUES

22 🅐 MAP P116, A3

For one of London's oddest shopping experiences, pass through security and descend 12m into the windowless subterranean depths of the London Silver Vaults, which house the largest collection of silver for sale in the world. The 30-odd independently owned shops, each entered through thick bank-safe-style doors, offer vintage Victorian and Georgian silver, cufflinks, candleholders, goblets and more. (https://silvervaultslondon.com)

Walking Tour 🥾

Tower of London to the Tate Modern

Commencing at one of London's most historic sights, this walk crosses the Thames on magnificent Tower Bridge before heading west along the river, scooping up some excellent views and passing breathtaking modern architecture, history and Shakespeare's Globe on the way. It comes to a halt amid the renowned contemporary artworks of the Tate Modern.

Walk Facts

Start Tower of London;
Ⓤ Tower Hill

End Tate Modern;
Ⓤ Southwark

Length 2.17 miles; 1½ hours

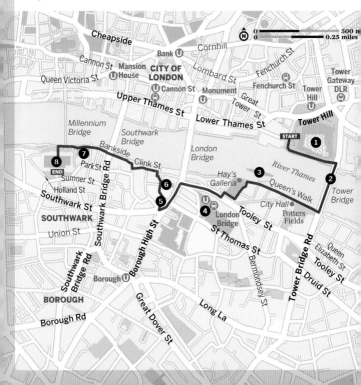

❶ Tower of London

The ancient **Tower of London** (p112) contains the oldest still-standing structure in the city, built in the 1070s. Be dazzled by the Crown Jewels, inlaid with the largest diamonds in the world, and tag along with a Yeoman Warder on an enlightening and entertaining tour.

❷ Tower Bridge

Cross ornate 19th-century **Tower Bridge** (p120) to the south side of the Thames. The bridge still raises, although these days it's powered electrically, instead of by steam, and shuts down traffic mainly for pleasure craft.

❸ HMS Belfast

Head down the stairs and walk west along the riverside Queen's Walk past City Hall. Moored a bit further ahead, **HMS Belfast** (p138), a light cruiser that served in WWII and later conflicts, is a floating museum.

❹ Shard

Stroll through the enclosed-dock-turned-shopping-complex of Hay's Galleria to Tooley St to see the **Shard** (p137), one of the tallest buildings in Europe.

❺ Borough Market

Continue west along Tooley St and dip south to **Borough Market** (p136), overflowing with small shops, food stalls and wholesale greengrocers catering to London's top-end restaurants.

❻ Southwark Cathedral

Southwark Cathedral (p136) is both fascinating and relaxing. Parts of the church date from medieval times, but its interior is beautifully Gothic, lined with pointed arches down the long nave and a 16th-century saint-filled High Altar Screen.

❼ Shakespeare's Globe

Wander west along Clink St – and past the remains of Winchester Palace – to Bankside and on to **Shakespeare's Globe** (p143). Join one of the informative tours or book tickets for a later show.

❽ Tate Modern

About 100m west of Shakespeare's Globe is the **Millennium Bridge** (p138) and London's standout modern- and contemporary-art gallery, the **Tate Modern** (p130).

✖ Take a Break

Borough Market's takeaway food stalls cluster in **Green Market**, close to Southwark Cathedral; fill up on anything from sizzling gourmet German sausages to Ethiopian curries and Caribbean stews. For a sit-down meal, try one of the many restaurants on the market fringes, such as **Arabica Bar & Kitchen** (p139) or **Padella** (p139).

Explore 🧭

Tate Modern & South Bank

South Bank is a must-visit area for art lovers, theatre-goers and architecture buffs, with the visionary Tate Modern and iconic brutalist buildings to explore. Come for the Thames views, great food markets, dollops of history, a smattering of street culture, and some excellent pubs, bars and restaurants on and around the riverfront.

The Short List

○ **Tate Modern (p130)** *Getting a grip on modern art by exploring this magnificent collection inside a former power station.*

○ **Shakespeare's Globe (p143)** *Garnering a Bard's-eye view of Elizabethan theatrics at this authentic re-creation of the 16th-century original.*

○ **Borough Market (p136)** *Stimulating your taste buds on a gastronomic tour of a gourmet market and its surrounding bars and restaurants.*

○ **Imperial War Museum (p136)** *Hearing the challenging stories behind conflicts past and present.*

Getting There & Around

Ⓤ The Jubilee Line is the main artery through South Bank, but the area can also be reached on the Bakerloo, Northern and Waterloo and City lines.

🚌 The RV1 bus runs from Tower Gateway to Covent Garden via South Bank and Bankside, linking the main sights.

⛴ Uber Thames Clippers boats stop at London Bridge City Pier, Bankside Pier and London Eye Pier.

Tate Modern & South Bank Map on p134

Tate Modern (p130) COWARDLION/SHUTTERSTOCK ©

Top Experience 📷

Get with the Trends at Tate Modern

Tate Modern is a phenomenally successful modern- and contemporary-art gallery housed in an imposing former power station on the riverside. Its exhibitions regularly make headlines and often sell out – with good reason.

◉ MAP P134, D2

📞 020-7887 8888

www.tate.org.uk

Bankside

admission free

🕐 10am-6pm Sun-Thu, to 10pm Fri & Sat

Ⓤ Southwark

Natalie Bell Building

The original gallery lies inside what was once the boiler house for the Bankside Power Station. Now called the Natalie Bell Building in recognition of a local community activist, the structure is an imposing sight: a 200m-long building made of 4.2 million bricks. Don't miss the views of the River Thames and St Paul's Cathedral from the 6th-floor cafe.

Turbine Hall

The first space to greet you as you pour down from the side entrance at Holland St is the astounding 3300-sq-metre Turbine Hall. Originally housing the power station's humongous electricity generators, this vast area has become the commanding venue for large-scale installations and temporary exhibitions. The annual commission aims to make art more accessible and has led to popular and often interactive pieces, such as Kara Walker's *Fons Americanus*, a 13m-tall working fountain that highlights the history of the slave trade; a full-on playground of three-person swings installed by Danish art collective Superflex; and a maze of geometric gardens called *Empty Lot* by Abraham Cruzvillegas, which took soil from parks around London and then watered it for six months to see if anything grew. Note that if you enter from the riverside doors, you'll end up on the more muted level 1, but stairs lead down to the main floor of the Turbine Hall.

Blavatnik Building

The Tate Modern extension that opened in 2016 echoes the original building in appearance: it is also constructed of brick, although these are slightly lighter and have been artistically laid out in a lattice to let light in (and out – the building looks stunning after dark).

The interior is stark, with raw, unpolished concrete vaguely reminiscent of brutalist

★ Top Tips

o The Natalie Bell Building and the Blavatnik Building are connected at levels 0, 1 and 4; pick up a map (£1) at one of the stands near the entrances to make navigating easier.

o For the most scenic of culture trips, take the RB2 Uber Boat service between **Bankside Pier** (www.thamesclippers.com) outside Tate Modern and **Millbank Pier** near its sister museum, Tate Britain (p62).

✕ Take a Break

Borough Market (p136), London's most fabulous food market, is a 10-minute walk east along the river. For a splendid sit-down meal, try hip Israeli kitchen Bala Baya (p140).

buildings, and the exhibition space is fantastic, giving the collection the room it deserves to breathe and shine.

Viewing Gallery: Level 10

Take the lift to level 10 for sweeping panoramic views of the city. The combination indoor-outdoor space means it's still worth a visit in bad weather. Note that the viewing gallery closed during the pandemic and had yet to reopen at the time of writing.

The Tanks

Huge subterranean tanks once stored oil for the power station, and these unusual circular spaces are now dedicated to showing live art, performance, installation and film.

Permanent Collection

Tate Modern's permanent collection is free to visit and is arranged by both theme and chronology on levels 2 and 4 of the Natalie Bell Building and on levels 0, 3 and 4 of the Blavatnik Building. The emphasis in the latter is on art from the 1960s onwards.

More than 60,000 works are on constant rotation, which can be frustrating if you'd like to see one particular piece, but keeps it thrilling for repeat visitors. Helpfully, you can check the excellent website (www.tate.org.uk/search) to see whether a specific work is on display – and where.

Curators have at their disposal paintings by Georges Braque, Henri Matisse, Piet Mondrian, Andy Warhol, Mark Rothko and Jackson

Tate Modern Viewing Gallery

Pollock, as well as pieces by Joseph Beuys, Barbara Hepworth, Damien Hirst, Rebecca Horn and Claes Oldenburg.

A great place to begin is the **Start Display** on level 2 of the Natalie Bell Building: this small, specially curated taster features some of the best-loved works in the collection and gives visitors useful pointers for understanding modern art.

Tours

Three free 45-minute tours run every day through Tate Modern's permanent exhibitions, providing an introduction to the gallery before moving on to a specific section. These talks start at noon, 1pm and 2pm on level 2 of the Natalie Bell Building.

Special Exhibitions

With the opening of the Blavatnik Building, Tate Modern has increased the number of special exhibitions it hosts. You will find the exhibits on level 3 of the

Tate of the Art

Swiss architects Herzog & de Meuron scooped the prestigious Pritzker Architecture Prize for their transformation of the empty Bankside Power Station, which closed in 1981. Strokes of genius included leaving the building's single central 99m-high chimney, adding a two-storey glass box onto the roof and using the cavernous Turbine Hall as a dramatic exhibition space. They also designed the Tate extension, the Blavatnik Building, which opened in 2016.

Natalie Bell Building and levels 2 and 4 of the Blavatnik Building; all are subject to admission charges, which vary by exhibition.

Past special exhibitions have included retrospectives on Andy Warhol, Henri Matisse, Edward Hopper, Frida Kahlo, Roy Lichtenstein, August Strindberg, Nazism and 'Degenerate art', and Joan Miró.

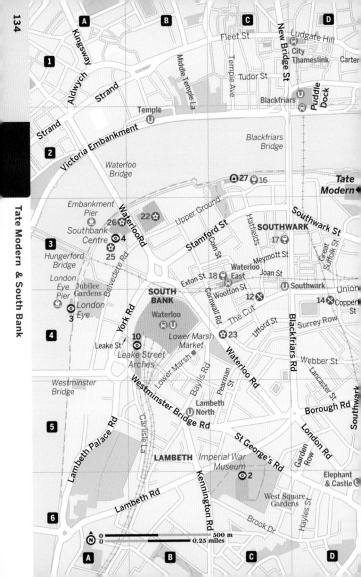

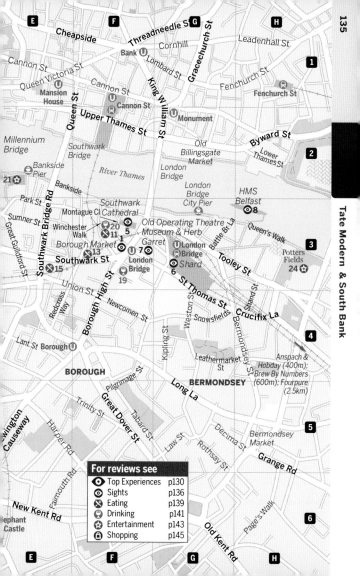

E

Cheapside

Cannon St

Queen Victoria St

Mansion House

Queen St

Upper Thames St

Millennium Bridge

21 Bankside Pier

Park St

Bankside

Sumner St

Great Guildford St

Montague Cl

Winchester Walk

Borough Market

13

15

Southwark St

Union St

Redcross Way

Lant St Borough U

BOROUGH

Pilgrimage St

Harper Rd

Trinity St

Great Dover St

Fanmouth Rd

New Kent Rd

ephant Castle

F

Threadneedle S

Bank U

Cannon St

Cannon St

Southwark Bridge

River Thames

Southwark Cathedral

20

11

5

1

7

London Bridge

19

Borough High St

Newcomen St

G

Cornhill

Lombard St

King William St

Monument U

Old Billingsgate Market

London Bridge

London Bridge City Pier

Old Operating Theatre Museum & Herb Garret

London Bridge U

6 St Thomas St

Weston St

Snowsfields

Kipling St

Leathermarket St

BERMONDSEY

Long La

Tabard St

Law St

Rothsay St

Old Kent Rd

H

1

Leadenhall St

Fenchurch St

Fenchurch St U

Byward St

2

Lower Thames St

HMS Belfast

8

Queen's Walk

3

Potters Fields

24

Tooley St

Battle Br La

Shard

Crucifix La

Bermondsey St

Shand St

Anspach & Hobday (400m); Brew By Numbers (600m); Fourpure (2.5km)

4

Decima St

Bermondsey Market

5

Grange Rd

Page's Walk

6

Gracechurch St

For reviews see

◉	Top Experiences	p130
◉	Sights	p136
✕	Eating	p139
🍷	Drinking	p141
✿	Entertainment	p143
🛍	Shopping	p145

Sights

Borough Market   MARKET

1 ⊙ MAP P135, F3

For a thousand years, a market has existed at the southern end of London Bridge, making this still-busy ancient gathering point a superb spectacle. Overflowing with small shops, food stalls cooking in close quarters and wholesale greengrocers catering to London's top-end restaurants, Borough Market makes a delicious lunch stop, afternoon grazing session or pure dinner-party inspiration. Expect it to be crowded, even on days with limited traders. (https://borough market.org.uk)

Imperial War Museum   MUSEUM

2 ⊙ MAP P134, C6

Fronted by an intimidating pair of 15in naval guns and a piece of the Berlin Wall, this riveting, state-of-the-art museum is housed in what was the Bethlem Royal Hospital, a psychiatric facility also known as Bedlam. The museum's focus is on WWI and WWII, which each have a dedicated gallery. The museum puts great emphasis on storytelling through individual testimonies, which are often as enlightening as they are poignant. (www.iwm.org.uk)

London Eye   VIEWPOINT

3 ⊙ MAP P134, A4

Standing 135m high in a fairly flat city, the London Eye is the world's largest cantilevered observation wheel and affords views 25 miles in every direction (as far as Windsor Castle), weather permitting. Each ride – or 'flight' – takes a gracefully slow 30 minutes. The London Eye is the focal point of the capital's midnight New Year's Eve fireworks display and one of the UK's most popular tourist attractions; book tickets online in advance for a slight discount or fast-track entry to jump the queue. (www.londoneye.com)

Southbank Centre   ARTS CENTRE

4 ⊙ MAP P134, A3

Southbank Centre, Europe's largest space for performing and visual arts, is made up of three brutalist buildings that stretch across seven riverside hectares: Royal Festival Hall (p144), Queen Elizabeth Hall (p145) and **Hayward Gallery** (www.southbank-centre.co.uk/venues/hayward-gallery). With cafes, restaurants, shops and bars, this complex is always a hub of activity, from the singing lift up to the 6th floor to teenage skateboarders doing tricks in the Undercroft. In summer, the **fountains** on the terrace are a hit with youngsters. (www.southbank-centre.co.uk)

Southwark Cathedral   CATHEDRAL

5 ⊙ MAP P135, F3

Southwark Cathedral, a mostly Victorian construction but with a history dating back many centuries earlier, was the nearest church to what was once the only entry point into the city, London Bridge. The cathedral is relatively small, but the Gothic arched nave is impressive, as is the 16th-century saint-filled High Altar Screen. Tombs and memorials are scattered throughout (follow the one-way system), including the tomb of John Gower and an alabaster Shakespeare Memorial. Evensong takes place at 5.30pm on weekdays, 4pm on Saturdays and 3pm on Sundays. (www.cathedral. southwark.anglican.org)

Shard   VIEWPOINT

6 ⊙ MAP P135, G3

Puncturing the skies above London, the dramatic splinter-like form of the Shard has become an icon of the city and is one of the tallest buildings in Europe.

The scene from the 244m-high viewing platforms on floors 69 and 72 is like no other in town, but it comes at an equally lofty price; book online in advance for a discount. Premium tickets come with a good-weather guarantee, meaning you are able to return for free.

To take in the view for less, visit one of the building's restaurants or bars; you'll pay half the viewing-platform ticket price for a cocktail at Aqua Shard (p143), where the views are still spectacular. (www.theview fromtheshard.com)

Borough Market

Strolling South Bank

It's best to explore South Bank on foot; if you're pressed for time, allocate at least half a day to walk from Westminster Bridge to London Bridge along the River Thames, with stops at the London Eye (p136), Southbank Centre (p136), Tate Modern (p130), Shakespeare's Globe (p143) and Borough Market (p136).

Old Operating Theatre Museum & Herb Garret MUSEUM

7 ◎ MAP P135, F3

This unique museum, 32 steps up a spiral stairway in the tower of St Thomas Church (1703), is the unlikely home of Britain's oldest surviving operating theatre. Rediscovered in 1956, the attic was used by the apothecary of St Thomas' Hospital to store medicinal herbs. The museum looks at the horror of 19th-century medicine, all pre-anaesthetic and pre-antiseptic. You can browse the natural remedies, including snail water for venereal disease, and recoil at the fiendish array of amputation knives and blades. (www.oldoperatingtheatre.com)

HMS Belfast SHIP

8 ◎ MAP P135, H3

HMS *Belfast* is a magnet for kids of all ages. This large, light cruiser – launched in 1938 – served in WWII, helping to sink the Nazi battleship *Sand* shelling the Normandy coast on D-Day, and in the Korean War. Its 6in guns could bombard a target 12 miles distant. Displays offer great insight into what life on board was like, in peacetime and during military engagements. Excellent audio guides, included in the admission fee, feature anecdotes from former crew members. (www.iwm.org.uk/visits/hms-belfast)

Millennium Bridge BRIDGE

9 ◎ MAP P135, E2

The elegant steel, aluminium and concrete Millennium Bridge staples the south bank of the Thames, in front of Tate Modern, to the north bank, at Peter's Hill below St Paul's Cathedral. The low-slung frame designed by Sir Norman Foster and Anthony Caro looks spectacular, particularly when lit up at night, and the view of St Paul's from South Bank has become one of London's iconic images.

Leake Street Arches STREET

10 ◎ MAP P134, B4

A grungy road under Waterloo station seems an unlikely place to find art, theatre and restaurants, but Leake St is the latest of London's railway arches to get the redevelopment treatment. Opened by famous street artist Banksy in 2008, the walls of the 200m-long **Leake Street Tunnel** are covered from floor to ceiling with some seriously impressive spray-painted works, and new taggers turn up daily. Banksy's work is long gone, but you can watch today's artists painting over what was put up yesterday. (http://leakestreetarches.london)

Eating

Padella
ITALIAN £

Padella (see 1 ◉ Map 135, F3) is a small, energetic bistro specialising in handmade noodles, inspired by the owners' extensive culinary adventures. Come hungry for the best pasta this side of Italy. The portions are small, which means that you can (and should!) have more than one dish. Download the WalkIn app to join the queue virtually to dine here then head to the market or pub.

The dishes on offer are often switched up, but the menu main-stay of *pici cacio e pepe* is a must. (www.padella.co)

Arabica Bar & Kitchen
MIDDLE EASTERN £

11 🍽 MAP P135, F3

Set in a brick-lined railway arch, Arabica specialises in classic Middle Eastern favourites served meze-style, so round up a group to sample and share as many of the small plates as possible. Stars of the menu include creamy baba ganoush, made with perfectly smoked aubergine and saffron yogurt, and charcoal-grilled lamb kebabs. (www.arabicabarandkitchen.com)

Millennium Bridge

Anchor & Hope

GASTROPUB ££

12 MAP P134, C4

Started by former chefs from nose-to-tail pioneer St. JOHN (p121), the Anchor & Hope is a quintessential gastropub: elegant but not formal, serving utterly delicious European fare with a British twist. The menu changes daily, but it could include grilled sole served with spinach, or roast rabbit with green beans in a mustard-and-bacon sauce. (www.anchorandhopepub.co.uk)

Casa do Frango

PORTUGUESE ££

13 MAP P135, F3

Forget your notions of Nando's: Casa do Frango kicks peri-peri up a notch in its cool plant-filled upstairs space steps away from Borough Market (p136). Frango, Algarvian-style charcoal-grilled chicken brushed with peri-peri sauce, is the star of the menu, which also includes regionally flavoured sharing plates. Seek out the hidden door to the dimly lit speakeasy for after-dinner drinks. (www.casadofrango.co.uk)

Bala Baya

ISRAELI £££

14 MAP P134, D4

This two-level arch is a love letter to Tel Aviv, with a whitewashed curving Bauhaus-inspired interior and a menu that changes seasonally, with lots of fantastic choices for vegetarians and vegans. With an Israeli chef at the helm, expect playful takes on Mediterranean favourites. The

Flat Iron Square

homemade *gazoz* (old-fashioned Israeli soft drinks) are delicious: try the orange and lychee. (https://balabaya.co.uk)

Skylon BRITISH £££

Named after the original structure in this location for the 1951 Festival of Britain, Skylon (see 25 ⊕ Map p134, A3) brings the 1950s into the modern era, with retro-futuristic decor (cool then, cooler now) and a season-driven menu of contemporary British cuisine. But its biggest selling point might be the floor-to-ceiling windows that bathe you in magnificent views of the Thames and the city. (www.skylon-restaurant.co.uk)

Flat Iron Square FOOD HALL £

15 🍴 MAP 135, E3

This industrial-chic food court has set up home in the railway arches and commandeered the outside space. Food stalls include pizza, game burgers, Lebanese and Venezuelan. There is also a tap room to quench your thirst. Flat Iron also hosts events. (www.flatironsquare. co.uk)

Drinking

Lyaness COCKTAIL BAR

16 🚇 MAP P134, C2

The term mixologist is often overused but not in this case: Ryan Chetiyawardana, the brain behind Lyaness, regularly creates completely new ingredients – to wit, oyster honey or blood

Lower Marsh Market

The views from the South Bank are grand, and the sights mighty, but the riverside is clogged with chains when it comes to food. Instead, head inland to **Lower Marsh Market** (www.lowermarshmarket. com) for street food with attitude (and a bit of bric-a-brac too). Located in the heart of Waterloo, in an area that has yet to be fully regenerated, it is a breath of fresh air from the polished strip along the river. The market runs on weekdays only and serves the local office crowd, as well as savvy visitors. The stalls run the gamut of world cuisine, at very reasonable prices.

curaçao – from which he then creates a selection of new cocktails. If there was ever a place to let the staff guide you, this is it. There are stunning City views to boot. (https://lyaness.com)

Seabird ROOFTOP BAR

17 🚇 MAP P134, C3

South Bank's latest rooftop bar might also be its best. Atop the Hoxton Southwark hotel, sleek Seabird has palm-filled indoor and outdoor spaces where you can spy St Paul's from the comfort of your wicker seat. If you're hungry, seafood is the

Bermondsey Beer Mile

Going on for more than a decade now, London's craft-beer mania shows no sign of letting up. Some two dozen breweries and taprooms have established themselves along a disjointed 2-mile stretch of industrial railway arches. Most are working breweries and limit opening hours to the weekends. Set aside a Saturday to sample the best of the city's beer scene.

Favourite stops along the Bermondsey Beer Mile include **Anspach & Hobday** (www.anspachandhobday.com), which pours its flagship dark coffee-chocolate porter among a handful of others; ever-experimental **Brew By Numbers** (www.bbno.co), with its 'scientific' branding and penchant for exploring new styles and refashioning old ones; and the revamped taproom of **Fourpure** (www.fourpure.com), complete with suspended egg chairs, trailing vines and, of course, much to choose from on its 43 craft-beer taps.

speciality, and the bar claims London's longest oyster list. (https://seabirdlondon.com)

Kings Arms   PUB

18 🍴 MAP P134, C3

Set on old-school Roupell St, this charming backstreet neighbourhood boozer serves up a rotating selection of traditional ales and bottled beers. The front room has retained original features, such as the working fireplace in winter, and is very atmospheric. The farmhouse-style extension at the back of the pub serves decent Thai food. (www.thekingsarmslondon.co.uk)

George Inn   PUB

19 🍴 MAP P135, F3

This magnificent galleried coaching inn is the last of its kind in London. The building, owned by the National Trust, dates from 1677 and is mentioned in Charles Dickens' *Little Dorrit*. In the evenings, the picnic benches in the huge cobbled courtyard fill up (no reservations); otherwise, find a spot in the labyrinth of dark rooms and corridors inside. (www.nationaltrust.org.uk/george-inn)

Rake   PUB

20 🍴 MAP P135, F3

London's original craft beer bar, and still one of the best, Rake has an astonishing selection of suds, including rare brews impossible to find anywhere else in town. Guided by the helpful bar staff, you can't go wrong. It's a teensy place, and it's always busy; the decking outside is especially popular. (www.uttobeer.co.uk)

Aqua Shard
BAR

If you fancy lingering over the view from the Shard (p137) with a cocktail in hand, find your way up to the 31st floor and into this gorgeous three-storey bar and restaurant. The lofty ceiling at Aqua Shard (see 6 Map p135, G3) adds awe to the London panoramas shining through the high sloping glass walls. Note that there is a minimum spend of £25 per person after 6pm. (www.aquashard.co.uk)

Entertainment

Shakespeare's Globe
THEATRE

21 MAP P135, E2

One of the most famous playhouses in the world, Shakespeare's Globe will knock your theatrical socks off. This dutifully authentic reconstruction will transport theatre-goers back to Elizabethan times, with hard wooden seats and a central floor space open to the elements (cushions and ponchos are on sale). Groundling tickets are just £5 for every performance, but you're required to stand through it all. (www.shakespearesglobe.com)

Kings Arms

Like a Local in South Bank

Neighbourhood local The views are grand, but the riverside is clogged with chain pubs. Instead, head inland for locally loved back-street boozers, such as **Kings Arms** (p142).

Hotel bars Londoners aren't staying overnight, but you'll sure find them at hip hotel watering holes, such as **Lyaness** (p141) and Hoxton's **Seabird** (p141).

Abandoned arches London's once derelict railway arches are undergoing huge regeneration projects: seek out street art in the **Leake Street Arches** (p138) or follow the still-in-progress Low Line to the restaurants in the Old Union Yard Arches and **Flat Iron Square** (p141).

National Theatre   THEATRE

22 ⭐ MAP P134, B3

The nation's flagship theatre delivers up to 25 shows every year across its three venues inside this brutalist block. Even if you're not here for a show, you can explore the foyers, which contain a bookshop, restaurants, bars and exhibition spaces. Get behind the scenes on a tour (adult/child £15/10), including going backstage and a deep-dive into the building's architecture. (www.nationaltheatre.org.uk)

Old Vic   THEATRE

23 ⭐ MAP P134, C4

This 1000-seater nonprofit theatre celebrated its 200th season in 2018 and continues to bring eclectic programming occasionally bolstered by big-name actors, such as Daniel Radcliffe or Helen Hunt. (www.oldvictheatre.com)

Bridge Theatre   THEATRE

24 ⭐ MAP P135, H3

Opened in 2017 and London's first new major theatre in 80 years, Bridge Theatre seats 900 in a cool, modern space and focuses on new productions, with the occasional classic thrown in. (https://bridgetheatre.co.uk)

Royal Festival Hall   LIVE PERFORMANCE

25 ⭐ MAP P134, A3

The 2700-capacity Royal Festival Hall is one of the best places in London to hear modern and classical music, poetry and spoken-word performances. The hall has four resident orchestras, including the **London Philharmonic Orchestra** and the **London Sinfonietta**. (www.southbankcentre.co.uk/venues/royal-festival-hall)

Queen Elizabeth Hall

LIVE PERFORMANCE

26 ⭐ MAP P134, A3

Queen Elizabeth Hall has a full programme of gigs, talks, dance performances and music throughout the year, on a smaller scale than the nearby Royal Festival Hall that's also part of Southbank Centre (p136). The space reopened in 2018 after a three-year refurb. In summer, don't miss the plant-strewn cafe-bar on the roof. (www.southbankcentre.co.uk/venues/queen-elizabeth-hall)

Shopping

Suck UK

GIFTS & SOUVENIRS

27 🔒 MAP P134, C2

Suck UK's arty, quirky gifts are so funny that you'll want to keep them for yourself. London's weather will likely call for an umbrella that changes colour

Royal Festival Hall

when wet, or you can pick up a few items for home, perhaps a cat scratcher that looks like a DJ turntable or a solar system coat rack. (www.suck.uk.com)

Explore ◎
Kensington Museums

Well-groomed Kensington is among London's handsomest neighbourhoods. It has three fine museums – Victoria & Albert Museum, Natural History Museum, and Science Museum – plus excellent dining and shopping, graceful parklands and grand period architecture.

The Short List

○ **Victoria & Albert Museum (p148)** *Thumbing through an encyclopaedic A to Z of decorative and design works while admiring the astonishing architecture.*

○ **Natural History Museum (p152)** *Gaping at the awe-inspiring stonework and inexhaustible collection.*

○ **Science Museum (p158)** *Grappling with the complexities of the world and the cosmos in this electrifying museum.*

○ **Hyde Park (p158)** *Picnicking in London's green lung and exploring its sights and verdant scenery.*

○ **Harrods (p166)** *Indulging in big-time shopping – or just big-time window-shopping!*

Getting There & Around

Ⓤ Get off at Hyde Park Corner, Knightsbridge and South Kensington (Piccadilly Line) and South Kensington, Sloane Sq and High St Kensington (Circle & District Lines).

🚌 Handy routes include 74, 52 and 360.

Kensington Museums Map on p156

Hyde Park (p158) ANTON_IVANOV/SHUTTERSTOCK ©

Top Experience 📷
Stroll among Artworks at Victoria & Albert Museum

Specialising in decorative art and design, the V&A's unparalleled collection is displayed in a setting as inspiring as the sheer diversity and rarity of its exhibits. Its original aims were the 'improvement of public taste in design' and 'applications of fine art to objects of utility'. In this endeavour, the museum continues to wow, astonish and inform.

◎ MAP P157, E5

V&A

www.vam.ac.uk

Cromwell Rd

admission free

🕑 10am-5.45pm Sat-Thu, to 10pm Fri

Ⓤ South Kensington

Collection

Through 146 galleries, the museum houses the world's greatest collection of decorative arts, from ancient Chinese ceramics to modernist architectural drawings, Korean bronze and Japanese swords, cartoons by Raphael, gowns from the Elizabethan era, ancient jewellery, a Sony Walkman – and much, much more. The museum is open till 10pm on Friday evenings, although the number of open galleries is reduced.

Entrance

Enter under the stunning blue-and-yellow blown-glass chandelier by Dale Chihuly. (If the 'Grand Entrance' on Cromwell Rd is too busy, enter around the corner on Exhibition Rd, or from the tunnel in the basement, if arriving by Tube.)

Level 0

The street level is mostly devoted to art and design from India, China, Japan, Korea and Southeast Asia, as well as European art. One of the museum's highlights is the **Cast Courts** in rooms 46a and 46b, containing staggering plaster casts collected in the Victorian era, such as Michelangelo's David, acquired in 1858. More European excellence is on display in room 48a in the form of the **Raphael Cartoons**.

The **TT Tsui (China) Gallery** (rooms 44 and 47e) displays lovely pieces, including a beautifully lithe wooden statue of Guanyin (a Mahayana bodhisattva) seated in a regal *lalitasana* pose from 1200 CE. Within the subdued lighting of the **Japan Gallery** (room 45) stands a fearsome suit of armour in the Domaru style. More than 400 objects are within the **Islamic Middle East Gallery** (room 42), including ceramics, textiles, carpets, glass and woodwork from the 8th century up to the years before WWI. The exhibition's highlight is the gorgeous mid-16th-century **Ardabil Carpet**. Soft lights illuminate the carpet on the hour and every half hour.

★ Top Tips

o Visit late on Friday nights, when there are fewer visitors.

o Work out what you want to see and how to reach it before you visit.

o Grab a museum map (£1 suggested donation) from the information desk.

o On a hot day, you'll find children splashing in the fountains.

✕ Take a Break

Perfect for a breather, the V&A Cafe (p164) is a picture; afternoon tea is a choice occasion.

For top-notch coffee and a bite to eat, head to **Farm Girl** (www.thefarmgirl.co.uk) on the pedestrianised section around the corner from South Kensington Tube station.

John Madejski Garden & Refreshment Rooms

The landscaped John Madejski Garden is a lovely shaded inner courtyard. Cross it to reach the original Refreshment Rooms (Morris, Gamble and Poynter Rooms), dating from the 1860s and redesigned by McInnes Usher McKnight Architects (MUMA), who also renovated the **Medieval and Renaissance galleries** (1350–1600) to the right of the Grand Entrance.

Level 1 & 3

The **British Galleries**, featuring every aspect of British design from 1500 to 1900, are divided between levels 2

John Madejski Garden

(1500–1760) and 4 (1760–1900). Level 4 also boasts the **Architecture Gallery** (rooms 127 to 128a), which vividly describes architectural styles via models and videos, and the spectacular, brightly illuminated **Contemporary Glass Gallery** (room 129).

Level 2

The **Jewellery Gallery** (room 91) is outstanding; the mezzanine level – accessed via the glass-and-perspex spiral staircase – glitters with jewel-encrusted swords, watches and gold boxes. The **Photographs Centre** (rooms 100 and 101) is one of the nation's best, with access to over 500,000 images collected since the mid-19th century. **Design Since 1945** (room 76) celebrates design classics from a 1985 Sony credit-card radio to a 1992 Nike 'Air Max' shoe, Peter Ghyczy's Garden Egg Chair from 1968 and the now ubiquitous selfie stick.

Level 4

Among the pieces in the **Ceramics Gallery** (rooms 136 to 146) are standout items from the Middle East and Asia. The **Dr Susan Weber Gallery** (rooms 133 to 135) celebrates furniture design over the past six centuries.

Temporary Exhibitions

The temporary exhibitions – covering anything from African fashion retrospectives to photography, illustration and design – are compelling and fun (admission fees apply). There are also talks, workshops and one of the best museum shops around.

V&A Through the Ages

The V&A opened in 1852 on the back of the runaway success of the Great Exhibition of 1851 and Prince Albert's enthusiasm for the arts. Its aims were to make art available to all, and to effect 'improvement of public taste in design'. It began with objects first collected by the Government School of Design in the 1830s and '40s and £5000 worth of purchases from the Great Exhibition profits.

Early Expansion

The Museum of Manufactures, as it was then known, moved to a collection of semi-permanent buildings in South Kensington in 1857. An expansion brought more ad hoc structures, and in 1890 the museum's board launched a competition to design the museum's new facade on Cromwell Rd and bring harmony to its architectural hotchpotch. Young architect Aston Webb (who went on to design the facade of Buckingham Palace) won, and Queen Victoria laid the foundation stone in May 1899. The occasion marked a name change, becoming the Victoria & Albert Museum.

Scrapping Admission Charges

When militant suffragettes threatened to damage exhibits at public museums in 1913, the V&A considered denying women entry to the museum, but instead opted for scrapping admission charges to the museum to boost visitor numbers and so help protect the V&A's collection.

V&A in the Wars

The V&A remained open during both world wars. When WWI broke out, several of French sculptor Auguste Rodin's works were on loan at the V&A and the hostilities prevented their return to France. Rodin was so moved by the solidarity of English and French troops that he donated the pieces to the museum. During WWII the museum was hit repeatedly by German bombs (a commemorative inscription remains on Cromwell Rd). Much of the collection had been evacuated (or, as with Raphael's cartoons, bricked in), so damage was minimal.

V&A Tours

Free volunteer-led guided highlights tours leave the main reception area every day at 10.30am and 2pm. Check the website for details of other, more specific, tours.

Exhibition Road Building Project

The Exhibition Road Building Project opened a magnificent new entrance leading to a courtyard, as well as the subterranean **Sainsbury Gallery**, a vast new venue for exhibitions.

Top Experience 📷
Explore Nature at the Natural History Museum

This colossal landmark is infused with the Victorian spirit of collecting, cataloguing and interpreting the natural world. A symphony in stone, the main museum building, designed by Alfred Waterhouse in blue and sand-coloured brick and terracotta, is as much a reason to visit as the world-famous collection within. Kids are the number-one fans, but adults also are enamoured of the exhibits.

◎ MAP P156, D5

www.nhm.ac.uk

Cromwell Rd

admission free

🕐 10am-5.50pm

👤

Ⓤ South Kensington

Architecture

Be sure to admire the astonishing architecture of Alfred Waterhouse. With carved pillars, animal bas-reliefs, sculptures of plants and beasts, leaded windows and sublime arches, the museum is a work of art and a labour of love.

Hintze Hall

When entering the museum's grand main entrance, this impressive central hall resembles a cathedral nave – fittingly, as it was built in a time when natural sciences were challenging Christian orthodoxy. Naturalist, first superintendent of the museum, and coiner of the word 'dinosaur' Richard Owen celebrated the building as a 'cathedral to nature'.

After 81 years in the Mammals Hall, the blue whale skeleton – Hope – was relocated to Hintze Hall, with the famous cast of a diplodocus skeleton (nicknamed Dippy) making way for the colossal marine mammal. The transfer itself was a mammoth and painstaking engineering project: disassembling and preparing 4.5-tonnes of bones for reconstruction in a dramatic diving posture that greets museum visitors.

Green Zone

While children love the Blue Zone, adults may prefer the Green Zone, especially the Treasures in the **Cadogan Gallery** (1st floor), which houses the museum's most prized possessions, each with a unique history. Exhibits include a chunk of moon rock, an Emperor Penguin egg collected by Captain Scott's expedition and a first edition of Charles Darwin's *On the Origin of Species*. Equally rare and exceptional are the gems and rocks held in the **Vault**, including a Martian meteorite and the largest emerald ever found. Pause to marvel at the trunk section of a 1300-year-old **giant sequoia tree** (2nd floor): its size is mind-boggling.

★ **Top Tips**

o Book for special events from yoga to sleepovers or a New year's Eve disco to enjoy an almost-empty museum.

o Check out the schedule of talks, special tours (like Women in Science), and sessions for neurodiverse visitors.

o Prebook your (free) tickets to guarantee entry.

o If you're arriving first thing in the morning, head to the Dinosaur Gallery before it's inundated with visitors.

o Take an audio-guided tour narrated by Sir David Attenborough by downloading recordings from the NHM website.

✕ **Take a Break**

The museum has several decent cafes for refuelling. For a pint and tasty pub grub in a classic London mews, head to the newly refurbished Queen's Arms (p165).

Back on the ground floor, the superb **Creepy Crawlies Gallery** delves into insect life and whether they're our friends or foes (turns out they're both).

Blue Zone

Undoubtedly the museum's star attraction, the **Dinosaurs Gallery** takes you on an impressive walkway, past a dromaeosaurus (a small and agile meat eater) before reaching a roaring animatronic T-rex and then winding its way through skeletons, fossils, casts and other absorbing dinosaur displays.

Another highlight of this zone is the **Mammals Gallery**, with extensive displays on both living and extinct warm-blooded animals, including the giant, wombat-related diprotodon, the largest marsupial ever to live until it was wiped out around 25,000 years ago. Lest we forget we are part of the animal kingdom, the museum has dedicated a gallery to **Human Biology**, where you'll be able to understand more about what makes us tick (senses, hormones, our brain...).

Red Zone

This zone explores the ever-changing nature of our planet and the forces shaping it. The earthquake simulator (in the **Volcanoes and Earthquakes Gallery**), which re-creates the 1995 Kobe earthquake in a grocery store (of which you can see footage), is a favourite, as is the **From the Beginning Gallery**, which retraces Earth's history.

Natural History Museum exhibit

In **Earth's Treasury** find out more about our planet's mineral riches and their everyday uses: from jewellery to construction and electronics. Visitors can trace the evolution of our species in the **Human Evolution Gallery**, including an engrossing model of the face of Britain's oldest, almost complete *Homo sapiens* skeleton: Cheddar Man, who lived around 10,000 years ago.

Access to most of the Red Zone galleries is via **Earth Hall** and an escalator that disappears into a huge metal sculpture of the Earth. **Sophie** the stegosaurus, at the base, is the world's most complete stegosaurus.

Orange Zone

The **Darwin Centre** is the beating heart of the museum. The top two floors of the amazing 'cocoon' building are dedicated to explaining the museum's research – windows even allow you to see the researchers at work. To find out more, pop into the **Attenborough studio** for one of the weekly talks with museum scientists. The studio also shows films throughout the day.

Wildlife Garden

The museum has begun to transform its outdoor spaces, creating

Exhibitions

The museum hosts regular exhibitions (admission fees apply), some of them on a recurrent basis. A major fixture is autumn's **Wildlife Photographer of the Year** (www.nhm.ac.uk), with show-stopping images. See the website for details of other exhibitions, such as 2022's 'Our Broken Planet: How We Got Here and Ways to Fix It'.

a piazza in the eastern grounds and enlarging the Wildlife Garden, a slice of English countryside in SW7 encompassing a range of British lowland habitats, including a meadow with farm gates, a bee tree where a colony of honey bees fills the air, and a pond (don't be surprised if you spot the occasional real sheep). Creating a space for urban wildlife is also the reason the famous Christmas ice rink here is now a thing of the past.

Museum Shop

As well as the obligatory dinosaur figurines and animal soft toys, the museum's shop has a brilliant collection of children's books about nature, animals and dinosaurs. On the adult side, browse for beautiful jewellery and lovely stationery.

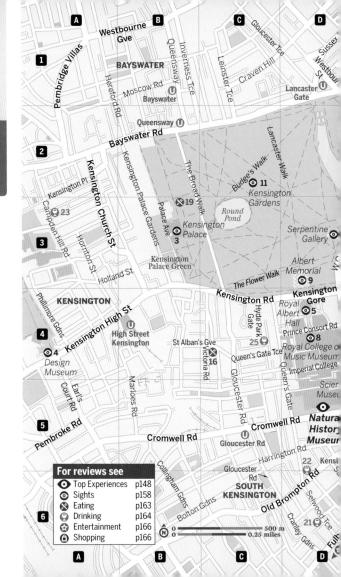

Westbourne Gve

Pembridge Villas

1

Queensway

Inverness Tce

BAYSWATER

Gloucester Tce

Craven Hill

Sussex

Westbourne

St

Moscow Rd

Bayswater U

Hereford Rd

Lancaster

Gate U

Leinster Tce

Queensway U

Bayswater Rd

2

Kensington Pl

Campden Hill Rd

Kensington Church St

Kensington Palace Gardens

The Broad Walk

Lancaster Walk

Budge's Walk

11

Kensington Gardens

23

Palace Ave

19

Round Pond

Serpentine Gallery

3

Hornton St

Kensington Palace

3

Kensington Palace Green

Holland St

Albert Memorial

9

The Flower Walk

KENSINGTON

Phillimore Gdns

Kensington High St

Kensington Rd

Kensington Gore

Royal Albert Hall

5

High Street Kensington U

Hyde Park Gate

4

Design Museum

Earl's Court Rd

Kensington High St

St Alban's Gve

Victoria Rd

16

25

Prince Consort Rd

8

Royal College of Music Museum

Queen's Gate Tce

Imperial College

4

Marloes Rd

Queen's Gate

Scien Museu

Gloucester Rd

Natura History Museu

5

Pembroke Rd

Cromwell Rd

Cromwell Rd U

Gloucester Rd U

Cromwell Rd

Harrington Rd

22 Kensi

Collingham Gdns

Gloucester Rd

SOUTH KENSINGTON

Old Brompton Rd

Selwood Tce

Bolton Gdns

21

Cranley Gdns

Full

For reviews see	
⊙ Top Experiences	p148
⊙ Sights	p158
⊗ Eating	p163
⊖ Drinking	p164
⊕ Entertainment	p166
⊕ Shopping	p166

N

0 — 500 m
0 — 0.25 miles

A   B   C   D

E Connaught St Edgware Rd F Seymour St G Oxford St H New Bond St 1

Hyde Park St

Bayswater Rd

Marble Arch Marble Arch 10

Duke St

Brook St

Grosvenor St

The Ring
North Ride

Speakers'
Corner

Park St

North Audley St

South Audley St

Mount St

Charles St 2

2
Hyde
Park

Park La

Curzon St

Hertford St

Piccadilly

The Serpentine

Serpentine Rd

Apsley
House 6

Green
Park 3

Rotten Row

12 Wellington
Arch

Buckingham
Palace
Gardens

Knightsbridge S Carriage Dr 15 Knightsbridge Knightsbridge

Hyde
Park
Corner

Grosvenor Pl 4

KNIGHTSBRIDGE

Ennismore
Gdns

Rutland Gate

Brompton Rd 28 24

Lowndes St

Sloane St

Belgrave
Sq

Belgrave Sq

Hobart Pl

Grosvenor
Gardens

Victoria & Albert Museum 29

Beauchamp Pl

Pont St

Eaton Pl

Victoria

Thurloe
Pl

Walton St

Cadogan Sq

Eaton Sq Eaton Sq

Buckingham
Palace Rd 5

Thurloe St

Milner St

Sloane St

Elizabeth St

South Eaton Pl

Fulham Rd 30

20

Eaton Tce

Victoria
Coach
Station

CHELSEA

Draycott Ave
Sloane Ave

Draycott Pl 31

King's Rd 14

Sloane Sq 26 Sloane Sq

Lower Sloane St

Warwick
Way 6

Astell St

Elystan Pl

Saatchi
Gallery

Pimlico Rd

Ebury Bridge Rd

Sydney St

Cale St

17

13

King's
Road

Royal
Hospital Rd

Chelsea Bridge Rd

E F G H

Speakers' Corner

Frequented by Karl Marx, Vladimir Lenin, George Orwell and William Morris, **Speakers' Corner** in the northeastern corner of Hyde Park is traditionally the spot for oratorical flourishes and soapbox ranting. If you've got something to get off your chest, do so on Sunday, although you'll mainly have fringe dwellers, religious fanatics and hecklers for company.

It's the only place in Britain where demonstrators can assemble without police permission, a concession granted in 1872 after serious riots 17 years before when 150,000 people gathered to demonstrate against the Sunday Trading Bill before Parliament, only to be unexpectedly ambushed by police concealed within Marble Arch. Some historians also link Speakers' Corner with the nearby Tyburn gallows, where condemned criminals might speak to the crowd before being hanged.

Sights

Science Museum
MUSEUM

1 ◉ MAP P156, D4

This scientifically spellbinding museum will mesmerise adults and children alike, with its interactive and educational exhibits covering everything from early technology to space travel. On the ground floor, a perennial favourite is **Exploring Space**, a gallery featuring genuine rockets and satellites and a full-size replica of the *Eagle,* the lander that took Neil Armstrong and Buzz Aldrin to the moon in 1969. The **Making the Modern World Gallery** next door is a visual feast of locomotives, planes, cars and other revolutionary inventions. (www.sciencemuseum.org.uk)

Hyde Park
PARK

2 ◉ MAP P157, F2

Hyde Park is central London's largest green space, expropriated from the church in 1536 by Henry VIII and turned into a hunting ground and later a venue for duels, executions and horse racing. The 1851 Great Exhibition was held here, and during WWII the park became an enormous potato field. These days, it's a place to stroll and picnic, boat on the **Serpentine lake**, or catch a summer concert or outdoor film during the summer months. (www. royalparks.org.uk/parks/hyde-park)

Kensington Palace
PALACE

3 ◉ MAP P156, B3

Built in 1605, Kensington Palace became the favourite royal residence under William and Mary of Orange in 1689, and remained so until George III became king and relocated to Buckingham Palace. Today it remains a residence for high-ranking royals. A large part of the palace is open to the public, however, including the King's and Queen's State Apartments. (www.hrp.org.uk/kensington-palace)

Design Museum   MUSEUM

4 ◉ MAP P156, A4

This slick museum is dedicated to design's role in everyday life. Its permanent collection is complemented by a revolving program of special exhibitions, and it's a crucial pit stop for anyone with an eye for recent technology or contemporary aesthetics. Splendidly housed in the refitted former Commonwealth Institute (which opened in 1962), the lavish interior – all smooth Douglas fir and marble – is itself a design triumph. (www.designmuseum.org)

Royal Albert Hall   HISTORIC BUILDING

5 ◉ MAP P156, D4

Built in 1871, thanks in part to the proceeds of the 1851 Great Exhibition organised by Prince Albert (Queen Victoria's husband), this huge, domed, red-brick amphitheatre, adorned with a frieze of Minton tiles, is Britain's most famous concert venue and home to the BBC's Promenade Concerts (the Proms) every summer. To find out about the hall's intriguing history and royal connections, and to gaze out from the Gallery, book an informative one-hour grand tour, operating most days. (www.royalalberthall.com)

Science Museum

Apsley House

HISTORIC BUILDING

6 ⊙ MAP P157, H3

This beautifully decorated Regency-era home was once the first building to appear when entering London from the west and was therefore known as 'No 1 London'. Today it contains exhibits about the Duke of Wellington, who defeated Napoleon Bonaparte at Waterloo. Memorabilia, including the Duke's death mask, fills the **basement gallery**, while an astonishing collection of china and silver, and paintings by Velasquez, Rubens, Van Dyck, Brueghel, Murillo and Goya awaits in the 1st-floor **Waterloo Gallery**, which runs the length of the building's west flank. (www.english-heritage.org.uk/visit/places/apsley-house)

Serpentine Gallery

GALLERY

7 ⊙ MAP P156, D3

This gallery, split over two sites, is one of London's most important contemporary-art galleries. Damien Hirst, Andreas Gursky, Louise Bourgeois, Gabriel Orozco, Tomoko Takahashi and Jeff Koons have all exhibited here. Each year a leading architect (who has never built in the UK) is commissioned to build a new 'Summer Pavilion' nearby: open to the public from June to October. The galleries run a full program of readings, talks and workshops. The Serpentine North Gallery, with a wing designed by Zaha Hadid Architects, is a few minutes away over the bridge. (www.serpentinegalleries.org)

Serpentine Gallery

Royal College of Music Museum

MUSEUM

8 ⊙ MAP P156, D4

From a collection of thousands of items spanning over 500 years of music history, 60 items have been selected for display here, including the earliest surviving guitar in the world. Many of the instruments are kept in playing condition and used in student performances. During the pandemic this illustrious museum was closed for a extensive refurbishment, reopening to the public in October 2021. (www.rcm. ac.uk/museum)

Albert Memorial

MONUMENT

9 ⊙ MAP P156, D3

This splendid Victorian confection on the southern edge of Kensington Gardens is as ostentatious as its subject wasn't. Queen Victoria's humble German husband Albert (1819–61) explicitly insisted he did not want a monument. Ignoring the good prince's wishes, the Lord Mayor instructed George Gilbert Scott to build the 53m-high, gaudy Gothic memorial. The 4.25m-tall gilded statue of the prince, surrounded by 187 figures representing the continents (Asia, Europe, Africa and America), the arts, industry and science, went up in 1876.

Marble Arch

MONUMENT

10 ⊙ MAP P157, F1

Designed by John Nash in 1828, this huge white arch was moved

here next to Speakers' Corner from its original spot in front of Buckingham Palace in 1851. If you're feeling anarchic, walk through the central portal, a privilege reserved by (unenforced) law for the Royal Family and the ceremonial King's Troop Royal Horse Artillery.

Lending its name to the neighbourhood, the arch contains three rooms (inaccessible to the public) and was a police station from 1851 to 1968 (two doors access the interior), large enough to accommodate 100 policemen who could rush to nearby Speaker's Corner if trouble was a-brewing. A ground **plaque** on the traffic island between Bayswater and Edgware Rds indicates the spot where the infamous Tyburn Tree, a three-legged gallows, once stood. An estimated 50,000 people were executed here between 1196 (the first recorded execution) and 1783, many having been dragged from the Tower of London. During the 16th century many Catholics were executed for their faith, and it later became a place of Catholic pilgrimage.

To the west of the arch stands a magnificent outsized bronze sculpture of a horse's head called *Still Water,* created by Nic Fiddian-Green in 2011.

Kensington Gardens

PARK

11 ⊙ MAP P156, C2

A delightful collection of manicured lawns, tree-shaded avenues and basins immediately west of Hyde Park, the picturesque expanse of Kensington Gardens is technically part of Kensington Palace (p158), located in the far west of the gardens. The large **Round Pond** in front of the palace is enjoyable to amble around, and also worth a look are the lovely fountains in the **Italian Gardens**, believed to be a gift from Prince Albert to Queen Victoria; they are now the venue of a cafe.

The **Diana, Princess of Wales Memorial Playground** in the northwest corner of the gardens has some pretty ambitious attractions for children. Next to the playground stands the delightful **Elfin Oak**, a 900-year-old tree stump carved with elves, gnomes, witches and small creatures. To the east, George Frampton's celebrated **Peter Pan statue** is close to the lake, while the opulent and elaborate Albert Memorial (p161) pokes into the sky south of Kensington Gardens, facing the Royal Albert Hall (p159). (www.royalparks.org.uk/parks/kensington-gardens)

Wellington Arch   MUSEUM

12 ◉ MAP P157, H3

Dominating the green space throttled by the Hyde Park Corner roundabout, this imposing neoclassical 1826 Corinthian arch originally faced the Hyde Park Screen, but was shunted here in 1882 for road widening. Once a police station, the arch today has four floors of galleries and temporary exhibition space as well as a permanent display about the history of the arch and a gift shop. The open-air balconies (accessible by lift) afford unforgettable views of Hyde Park, Buckingham Palace and the Mall. (www.english-heritage.org.uk/visit/places/wellington-arch)

King's Road   STREET

13 ◉ MAP P157, F6

At the counter-cultural forefront of London fashion during the technicolour '60s and anarchic '70s (Ian Fleming's fictional spy James Bond had a flat in a square off the road), the King's Rd today is more a stamping ground for the leisured shopping set. The last punks – once tourist sights in themselves – have long since departed. Today it's all snappily dressed locals perusing designer stores and the sprinkling of specialist shops. Nearby Pavilion Rd is an excellent detour for foodies.

Saatchi Gallery   GALLERY

14 ◉ MAP P157, G6

This grandly housed gallery in the Duke of York's Headquarters hosts temporary exhibitions of experimental and thought-provoking work across a variety of media, much of it international in nature. The white and sanded bare-floorboard galleries are magnificently presented, and the gallery shop is bursting with arty souvenirs and gifts to buy yourself. Check the website for details of current and forthcoming exhibitions (www.saatchigallery.com)

Eating

Dinner by Heston Blumenthal BRITISH £££

15 MAP P157, F3

With two Michelin stars, sumptuously presented Dinner is a gastronomic tour de force, taking diners on a journey through British culinary history (with inventive modern inflections). Dishes carry historical dates to convey context, while the restaurant interior is a design triumph, from the glass-walled kitchen and its overhead clock mechanism to the large windows looking onto the park. Book ahead. (www.dinnerbyheston.com)

Launceston Place BRITISH £££

16 MAP P156, C4

This exceptionally handsome, superchic Michelin-starred restaurant is almost anonymous on a picture-postcard Kensington street of Edwardian houses. Overseen by chef patron Ben Murphy, dishes occupy the acme of gastronomic pleasures and are accompanied by an award-winning wine list. The adventurous will aim for the seven-course tasting menu (£95; vegetarian and vegan versions available). (www. launcestonplace-restaurant.co.uk)

Peter Pan statue in Kensington Gardens (p161)

Rabbit   BRITISH ££

17 🍴 MAP P157, F6

Three brothers grew up on a farm. One became a farmer, another a butcher, while the third worked in hospitality. So they pooled their skills and came up with Rabbit, a breath of fresh air in upmarket Chelsea. The restaurant rocks the agri-chic look, with a creative, seasonal, oft-changing Modern British menu. The plant-based set lunch is great value. (www.rabbit-restaurant.com)

V&A Cafe   CAFE £

18 🍴 MAP P157, E4

There is plenty of hot and cold food to choose from at the V&A Cafe, and the setting is quite astonishingly beautiful: the extraordinarily decorated Morris, Gamble and Poynter Rooms (1868) show Victorian Classic Revival style at its very best – these were the first museums cafes in the world. Plus there's often a piano accompaniment to your tea and cake. (www.vam.ac.uk/info/va-cafe)

Orangery   CAFE ££

19 🍴 MAP P156, B3

Take afternoon tea (or breakfast, or lunch) in the grounds of a royal palace. The Orangery at the Kensington Palace Pavilion overlooks the Sunken Garden with its terraces of ornamental flower beds. The photo-worthy traditional English Afternoon Tea, which is served pretty much all day, is £38.00 per person (£19 for children). Throw in some Pimms or sparkling for £44 per person.

Wulf & Lamb   VEGAN £

20 🍴 MAP P157, G5

Picture-perfect Pavilion Rd, a side street tucked off Sloane Sq, has been redeveloped in recent years to create a village-like collection of independent, artisan retailers. Standing out amid the cheesemonger, butcher, coffee shop and many others is Wulf & Lamb, a vegan restaurant that offers an elegant setting for its animal-friendly menu. The restaurant is cashless. (www.wulfandlamb.com)

Drinking

Anglesea Arms   PUB

21 🍺 MAP P156, D6

Seasoned with age and decades of ale-quaffing patrons (including Charles Dickens, who lived on the same road, and DH Lawrence), this historic pub boasts considerable character, an excellent menu, and a strong showing of beers and gins. The terrace out the front swarms with punters in warmer months. The Sunday roast menu in winter includes a vegan option. (www.angleseaarms.com)

K Bar   COCKTAIL BAR

22 🍸 MAP P156, D5

In a part of town traditionally bereft of choice, the K Bar is a reassuring presence. It[s a hotel bar maybe, but don't let that stop you – the place exudes panache with its leather-panelled and green-marble-counter bar, smoothly glinting brass, oak walls and chandeliers, drawing a cashed-up crowd who enjoy themselves. Cocktails are prepared with as much class as the ambience. (www.townhousekensington.com/k-bar)

Windsor Castle PUB

23 MAP P156, A3

This classic tavern on the brow of Campden Hill Rd has history, nooks and charm on tap. Alongside a decent beer selection and a solid gastropub-style menu, it has a historic compartmentalised interior, a roaring fire (in winter), a delightful beer garden (in summer) and affable regulars (all seasons). In the old days, Windsor Castle was visible from the pub, hence the name. (www.thewindsorcastlekensington.co.uk)

Coffee Bar CAFE

24 MAP P157, F4

When your legs are turning to lead traipsing around Harrods, gravitate towards the shop's curvilinear Deco-style bar in the Roastery and Bake Hall for some decidedly smooth coffee at the heart of the shopping action. Come evening, it's all coffee negronis and chilled espresso martinis. Sittings are limited to 45 minutes. (www.harrods.com)

Hyde Park's Secret Pet Cemetery

An oddity by Victoria Gate on the north side of Hyde Park, this small boneyard for over one thousand dogs, cats and other pets was founded in 1881, before interring its last furry occupant in 1903. With its midget headstones commemorating legions of affectionately named moggies and mongrels, the cemetery can only be visited as part of the on the Hidden Stories of Hyde Park tours (£12) arranged by Royal Parks (www.royalparks.org.uk) on the third Friday of the month; check the website for details.

Queen's Arms PUB

25 MAP P156, C4

Just around the corner from the Royal Albert Hall is this blue-and-grey-painted godsend. Located in an adorable cobbled-mews setting off bustling Queen's Gate, the pub beckons with a cosy interior, welcoming staff and a right royal selection of ales – including selections from small, local cask brewers – and ciders on tap. In warm weather, drinkers stand outside in the mews (only permitted on one side). (www.thequeensarmskensington.co.uk)

Entertainment

Royal Albert Hall

CONCERT VENUE

26 ⭐ MAP P157, G5

This splendid Victorian concert hall hosts classical music, rock and other performances, but is famously the venue for the BBC-sponsored Proms. Booking is possible, but from mid-July to mid-September Promenaders queue for £5 standing tickets that go on sale one hour before curtain-up. Otherwise, the box office and prepaid-ticket collection counter are through door 12 (south side of the hall). (www.royalalberthall.com)

John Sandoe Books

Royal Court Theatre

THEATRE

27 ⭐ MAP P156, D6

Equally renowned for staging innovative new plays and old classics, the Royal Court is among London's most progressive theatres and has continued to foster major writing talent across the UK for over 60 years. There are two auditoriums: the main Jerwood Theatre Downstairs and the much smaller studio Jerwood Theatre Upstairs. (www.royalcourttheatre.com)

606 Club

BLUES, JAZZ

Named after its old address on the King's Rd, which cast a spell over London's jazz lovers back in the '80s, this choice, tucked-away basement jazz club and restaurant gives centre stage nightly to contemporary British-based jazz musicians. Nonmembers must be dining to be served alcohol, and it is advised to book ahead to get a table. (www.606club.co.uk)

Shopping

Harrods

DEPARTMENT STORE

28 🏢 MAP P157, F4

Garish and stylish in equal measure, perennially crowded Harrods is an obligatory stop for visitors, from the cash-strapped to the big spenders. The stock is astonishing, as are many of the price tags. Many visitors don't make it past the ground floor where designer bags, myriad scents from the perfume hall and the mouthwatering counters of the food hall provide plenty of entertainment. (www.harrods.com)

V&A Shop
ARTS & CRAFTS

29 🔒 MAP P157, E5

Before checking out of the V&A, stop by the ground-floor shop facing the Cromwell Rd entrance and rummage through a stirring and very sharp display of (impulse purchase) gifts, books, fabrics and prints, all design-oriented and inspired by exhibitions and iconic pieces at the museum, as well as a delightful range of jewellery from independent jewellery-makers. (www.vam.ac.uk/info/shopping-at-the-va)

Conran Shop
DESIGN

30 🔒 MAP P157, E5

The original design store (going strong since 1987), the Conran Shop is a treasure trove of beautiful things – from radios to sunglasses, kitchenware to children's toys, coffee-table books, and greeting cards. Browsing bliss. While you're here check out the magnificent Art-Nouveau Michelin House that houses the shop. (www.conranshop.co.uk)

Household Cavalry 👍

Catch the Household Cavalry departing for Horse Guards Parade at 10.30am (9.30am Sundays) from Hyde Park Barracks for the daily Changing the Guard (p64), performing a ritual that dates from 1660. They troop via Hyde Park Corner (and under Wellington Arch), Constitution Hill and the Mall. It's not as busy as the Changing the Guard at Buckingham Palace and you can get closer to the action.

John Sandoe Books
BOOKS

31 🔒 MAP P157, F6

Steeped in literary charm and a perfect antidote to impersonal book superstores, this three-storey bookshop in an 18th-century premises inhabits its own universe. A treasure trove of literary gems and hidden surprises, it's been in business for over six decades. Loyal customers swear by it, and knowledgeable booksellers spill forth with well-read pointers and helpful advice. (www.johnsandoe.com)

Kensington Museums Shopping

Walking Tour ⛷

A Saturday in Notting Hill

A Notting Hill Saturday sees the neighbourhood at its busiest and best. Buzzing Portobello Road Market radiates vibrant colour, and great neighboourhood restaurants, shops and an absorbing museum make the day an event that embraces market and shop browsing, culinary surprises, book-hunting and a chance to catch a film in a classic picture-house setting.

Getting There

U Notting Hill Gate station is on the Circle, District and Central Lines.

U Ladbroke Grove station on the Hammersmith & City and Circle Lines is also useful.

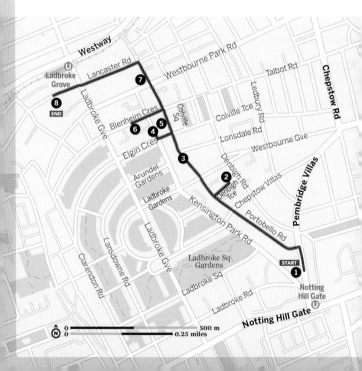

❶ Arancina

Close to Notting Hill Gate Tube station and en route to Portobello Market, you can't miss **Arancina** (www.arancina.co.uk) with its orange cut-out Fiat 500 in the window. It's a great spot for *arancine* (fried rice balls with fillings), freshly baked pizza, craft beer or a glass of red.

❷ Denbigh Terrace

Delve into Denbigh Terrace for its row of vibrantly painted terraced houses on the south side of the street, which make for a candy-coloured photo-op for the 'gram, especially if it's sunny.

❸ Portobello Road Market

Stroll along Portobello Rd until you reach the iconic **Portobello Road Market** (www.portobellomarket. org). The market mixes street food with fruit and veg, antiques, colourful fashion and iconic gifts.

❹ Lutyens & Rubinstein Bookshop

Divert left to visit **Lutyens & Rubinstein** (www.lutyensrubinstein. co.uk) bookshop. Its small size pays dividends. Established by a pair of literary agents, it focuses discerningly on 'excellence in writing', as determined by customers and readers.

❺ Electric Cinema

Wander back to Portobello Rd to the **Electric Cinema** (www. electriccinema.co.uk), one of the UK's oldest cinemas, with luxurious leather armchairs, footstools, sofas and even front-row double beds! Check the fabulous tiled floor interior.

❻ Blenheim Crescent

Turn left into Blenheim Cres for a string of browse-worthy shops, including glassware at **Ceramica Blue** (www.ceramicablue.co.uk) and the **Notting Hill Bookshop** (www. thenottinghillbookshop.co.uk), the inspiration behind the shop in Hugh Grant and Julia Roberts' classic 1999 rom-com *Notting Hill*.

❼ The Blue Door

Head back to Portobello Rd and turn north. When you reach the corner of Westbourne Park Rd, you might be wondering why everyone is taking selfies at that blue door. It's (a replica) of the famous *Notting Hill* scene when Hugh Grant opens the door to the paparazzi in his trunks, followed by his house-mate (played by Rhys Ifans) in his briefs. Maybe best not to re-enact this scene in winter.

❽ Museum of Brands

Finally, take a left at Lancaster Rd and head to the excellent **Museum of Brands** (www.museumof brands.com), which retraces the history of consumer culture. It'll amuse the kids and make the grown-ups nostalgic over the retro packaging and iconic products from days gone by.

Explore ◈

Regent's Park & Camden

Regent's Park, Camden Market and Hampstead Heath should top your list for excursions into North London. Camden is a major sight with an intoxicating energy and brilliant nightlife, while Regent's Park is an oasis of calm and sophistication amid the North London buzz. Meanwhile, Hampstead Heath offers you a glorious day out and an insight into how North Londoners spend their weekends.

The Short List

○ **Camden Market (p176)** Soaking up the frantic energy of this legendary market.

○ **Hampstead Heath (p176)** Enjoying the sweeping views of London from Parliament Hill.

○ **ZSL London Zoo (p176)** Meeting and communing with furred and feathered friends.

○ **Regent's Park (p177)** Exploring central London's largest and most elaborate Royal Park.

○ **Madame Tussauds (p177)** Ogling at idols (and otherwise) at the world's most celebrated waxworks.

Getting There & Around

Ⓤ For Regent's Park, Baker St (on the Jubilee, Metropolitan, Circle, Hammersmith & City and Bakerloo Lines) is most useful. The best stations for Camden are Camden Town and Chalk Farm on the Northern Line. Hampstead is also on the Northern Line.

Regent's Park & Camden Map on p174

Camden Market (p176) BLUE SKY IN MY POCKET/GETTY IMAGES ©

Walking Tour 🥾

Highlights of North London

Part of the appeal of North London is that it's a great area to just wander – in parks and markets and along canals. This itinerary takes in some of the most atmospheric spots, as well as the big-hitting sights. If you can, stay into the evening to enjoy Camden's fantastic live-music scene.

Walk Facts

Start Madame Tussauds;
Ⓤ Baker St

End Lock Tavern;
Ⓤ Chalk Farm

Length 2.5 miles; 2½ hours

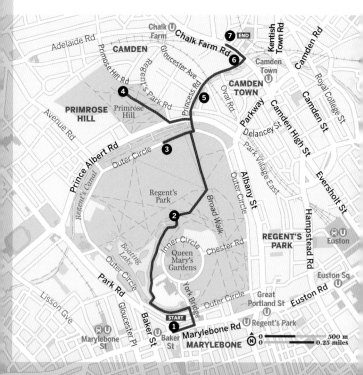

❶ Madame Tussauds

Make sure you pack your selfie stick for a chance to pose with your idols at this waxwork **museum** (p177) – there are plenty of personalities to ogle and (maybe) admire, from past and current statesmen to sportspeople, actors, singers and movie characters.

❷ Regent's Park

Walk along Marylebone Rd, turn left onto York Gate and head into **Regent's Park** (p177) over York Bridge. Follow the shores of the **boating lake** to explore the most scenic parts of the park before heading east and joining the **Broad Walk**, the park's main avenue.

❸ London Zoo

Explore London's famous **zoo** (p176), where enclosures have been developed to be as close to the animals' original habitats as possible – among the highlights are Land of the Lions, Gorilla Kingdom, In with the Lemurs, Tiger Territory and Penguin Beach.

❹ Views from Primrose Hill

Cross Regent's Canal and make your way towards the top of **Primrose Hill** for fantastic views of London's skyline. The park is very popular with families and picnickers at the weekend.

❺ Regent's Canal

Head back down Primrose Hill and join the picturesque **Regent's Canal** (p177) towpath for an easy stroll towards Camden. The path is lined with residential narrow boats, stunning houses and old warehouses converted into modern flats. Leave the towpath when you reach Camden Lock and its market.

❻ Camden Market

Browse the bags, clothes, jewellery and arts and crafts stalls of Camden's famous market. There are two main market areas, but they both sell more or less the same things. **Camden Lock Market** (p111) is the original; push into **Stables Market** (www.camdenmarket.com) for more rummaging.

❼ Lock Tavern

Settle in for a well-earned drink at the **Lock Tavern** (p180), and if the weather is good, sit on the roof terrace and watch the world go by. Check out what's on in the evening too, as the pub hosts regular bands and DJs.

✖ Take a Break

Few places are more scenic in London than the top of Primrose Hill: pack a picnic for lunch with the best view of the city. Alternatively, hold out until you make it to **Camden Market** (p176), where there are food stalls galore.

Regent's Park & Camden

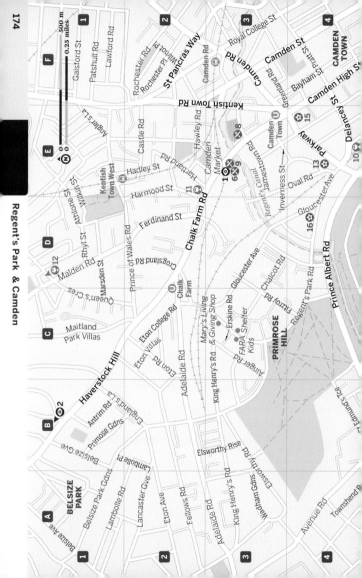

BELSIZE PARK

HAVERSTOCK HILL

PRIMROSE HILL

CAMDEN TOWN

Kentish Town West

Chalk Farm

Camden Town

Camden Market

Maitland Park Villas

Mary's Living & Giving Shop

FARA Shelter Kids

Royal College St

Camden St

Camden High S

Bayham St

Delancey St

St Pancras Way

Kentish Town Rd

Camden Rd

Rochester Rd

Rochester Pl

Wilmot Pl

Hawley Rd

Castle Rd

Hadley St

Harmood St

Ferdinand St

Chalk Farm Rd

Hartland Rd

Prince of Wales Rd

Crogsland Rd

Malden Rd

Marsden St

Queen's Cres

Athlone St

Wilkin St

Gaisford St

Patshull Rd

Lawford Rd

Angler's La

Regent's Canal

Jamestown Rd

Inverness St

Oval Rd

Gloucester Ave

Gloucester Cres

Chalcot Rd

Fitzroy Rd

Regent's Park Rd

Prince Albert Rd

Erskine Rd

Anger Rd

King Henry's Rd

Eton College Rd

Eton Villas

Eton Rd

Adelaide Rd

Elsworthy Rise

Wadham Gdns

Elsworthy Rd

King Henry's Rd

Avenue Rd

Townshend R

Edmund's Te

Belsize Ave

Belsize Gve

Primrose Gdns

Belsize Park Gdns

Lambolle Pl

Lambolle Rd

Lancaster Gve

Eton Ave

Fellows Rd

Adelaide Rd

England's La

Antrim Rd

500 m

0.25 miles

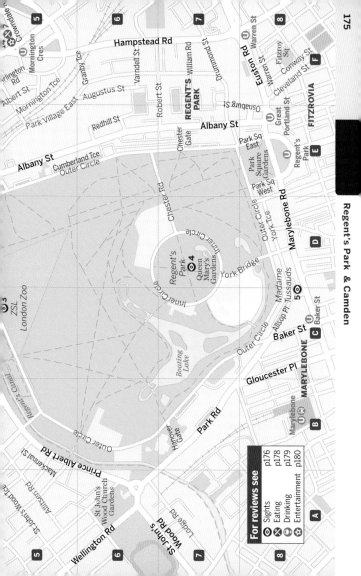

Regent's Park & Camden

Hampstead Rd

REGENT'S PARK

Albany St

Albany St

Cumberland Tce
Outer Circle

Mornington
Cres

Warren St

Euston Rd

Fitzroy
Sq

Conway St

Cleveland St

FITZROVIA

Great
Portland St

Regent's Park

FITZROVIA F

E

Park Sq
East

Park
Square
Gardens

Park Sq
West

Marylebone Rd

Outer Circle

York Tce

Marylebone Rd

D

Regent's
Park

Queen
Mary's
Gardens

York Bridge

Inner Circle

Madame
Tussauds

Baker St

C

Inner Circle

Allsop Pl

Baker St

MARYLEBONE

Gloucester Pl

Marylebone

Outer Circle

B

ZSL
London Zoo

Boating
Lake

Park Rd

Hanover
Gate

Regent's Canal

Outer Circle

Prince Albert Rd

MacKennal St

St John's
Wood Church
Gardens

St John's
Wood Rd

Wellington Rd

Lodge Rd

Alma Sq

St Johns Wood Tce

A

Crowndale
Rd

Mornington Tce

Arlington
Rd

Albert St

Park Village East

Augustus St

Redhill St

Granby Tce

Vardnell St

Robert St

Chester
Gate

Chester Rd

Hampstead Rd

William Rd

Drummond St

Warren St

Osnaburg St

Cleveland St

Walking along Regent's Canal

The canals that were once a trade lifeline for the capital have now become a favourite escape for Londoners, providing a quiet walk away from traffic and crowds. You can walk from Little Venice to Camden in less than an hour; on the way, you'll pass Regent's Park, London Zoo, Primrose Hill, beautiful villas designed by architect John Nash and old industrial buildings redeveloped into trendy blocks of flats. Allow 15 to 20 minutes between Camden and Regent's Park, and 25 to 30 minutes between Regent's Park and Little Venice. There are plenty of exits and signposts along the way.

Sights

Camden Market   MARKET

1 ◉ MAP P174, E3

Although – or perhaps because – it stopped being cutting-edge several million cheap leather jackets ago, Camden Market attracts millions of visitors each year and is one of London's most popular attractions. What started out as a collection of attractive craft stalls beside Camden Lock on the Regent's Canal now extends most of the way from Camden Town Tube station to Chalk Farm Tube station. (www.camdenmarket.com)

Hampstead Heath   PARK

2 ◉ MAP P174, B1

Sprawling Hampstead Heath (p182), with its rolling woodlands and meadows, feels a million miles away – despite being about 3.5 miles from Trafalgar Sq. It covers 320 hectares and is home to about 180 bird species, 25 species of butterflies, grass snakes, bats and

a rich array of flora. It's a wonderful place for a ramble, especially to the top of **Parliament Hill**, which offers expansive views across flat-as-a-pancake London. (www.cityoflondon.gov.uk/things-to-do/green-spaces/hampstead-heath)

ZSL London Zoo   ZOO

3 ◉ MAP P175, C5

Opened in 1828, London Zoo is the oldest in the world. The emphasis nowadays is firmly on conservation, breeding and education, with fewer animals and bigger enclosures. Highlights include Land of the Lions, Gorilla Kingdom, Tiger Territory (three cubs were born in summer 2022), Penguin Beach and the walk-through In with the Lemurs. There are regular feeding sessions and talks; various experiences are available, such as Keeper for a Day; and you can even spend the night in one of nine Gir Lion Lodge cabins. (www.zsl.org/zsl-london-zoo)

Regent's Park

PARK

4 ◉ MAP P175, D7

The largest and most elaborate of central London's many Royal Parks, Regent's Park is one of the capital's loveliest green spaces. Among its many attractions are London Zoo, **Regent's Canal** (https://canalrivertrust.org.uk/enjoy-the-waterways/canal-and-river-network/regents-canal), an ornamental lake, and sports pitches where locals meet to play football, rugby and volleyball. **Queen Mary's Gardens**, towards the south of the park, are particularly pretty, especially in June when the roses are in bloom. Performances take place here in an **open-air theatre** (www.openairtheatre.com) during summer. (www.royalparks.org.uk/parks/the-regents-park)

Madame Tussauds

MUSEUM

5 ◉ MAP P175, C8

It may be kitschy and pricey, but Madame Tussauds makes for a fun-filled day. There are photo ops with your dream celebrity (be it Daniel Craig, Lady Gaga, Benedict Cumberbatch or Audrey Hepburn), the Marvel set (Black Panther, Captain America, Iron Man etc) and the Royals (the late Queen Elizabeth II, King Charles III and the Queen Consort, Harry and Meghan, William and Kate). Book online for slightly cheaper rates and check the website for seasonal opening hours. (www.madame-tussauds.com/london)

Hampstead Heath

Heath Marvels

Hampstead Heath, which is managed by the City of London Corporation, is a little slice of countryside despite being in Zone 2.

It is a place to wander. Sandy Heath, for example, is like stepping into another world. Getting off the beaten track will give you the best chance of spotting wildlife too.

Swimming costumes are a must for a refreshing dip in one of our famous ponds. Just lay back and gaze at the sky as you swim among the trees. Just check the temperature first!

You should definitely pack a picnic too; find a shady spot in one of the wildflower meadows. There's so much to explore on the Heath – one visit is never enough!

By Jo Maddox, Conservation Ranger at Heath Hands

Eating

Chin Chin Labs   ICE CREAM £

6 ✕ MAP P174, E3

This is food chemistry at its absolute best. Chefs prepare the ice-cream mixture and freeze it on the spot by adding liquid nitrogen. Flavours change regularly and match the seasons (tonka bean, burnt-butter caramel or vegan banana ice-cream, for instance). The dozen toppings and sauces are equally creative. Try the ice cream sandwich (£5.95): ice cream wedged inside gorgeous brownies or cookies. (www.chinchinlabs.com)

Cafe KOKO   PIZZA £

7 ✕ MAP P175, F5

A bonus from the expansive refurbishment of the legendary KOKO (p180) music venue next door, Cafe KOKO takes its inspiration from New York–style 1930s eateries. Food is served from 8am to 1am, a rarity in London, from hearty breakfasts to excellent pizzas and hangover-saving sandwiches. The beautiful decor features art and photos from KOKO's, a nod to its long and illustrious history. (www.koko.co.uk/restaurants/cafe-koko)

Poppies

FISH & CHIPS ££

8 🍴 MAP P174, E3

The largest of the three branches of this high-vis chippy serves reliable fish (choose from a half-dozen types) and chips to up to 110 diners over two levels just opposite the major magnet that is Camden Market. Great decor too, with reclaimed (or repurposed) 1940s fixtures and fittings throughout. (https://poppiesfishandchips.co.uk)

Camden Market West Yard

INTERNATIONAL £

9 🍴 MAP P174, E3

There are dozens of food stalls at the West Yard of Camden Lock Market where you can find virtually every type of cuisine, from French to Argentinian, Japanese and Caribbean. Quality varies but is generally pretty good and affordable, and you can eat on the large communal tables, or by the canal. (www.camdenmarket.com)

Drinking

Edinboro Castle

PUB

10 🍺 MAP P174, E4

Large and relaxed, the Edinboro offers a fun atmosphere, a fine bar and a full menu. The highlight, however, is the huge beer garden, complete with warm-weather barbecues and decorated with festoons of lights on long summer evenings. Patio heaters appear in winter. (www.edinborocastlepub.co.uk)

Camden Market

Lock Tavern PUB

11 MAP P174, E2

A Camden institution, the black-clad Lock Tavern rocks: it's cosy inside, and it has a rear beer garden and a great roof terrace from where you can watch the market throngs. Beer is plentiful here and it proffers a prolific roll call of guest bands and well-known DJs at weekends to rev things up. Dancing is encouraged. Entry is always free. (www.lock-tavern.com)

Garden Gate PUB

12 MAP P174, D1

At the bottom of Hampstead Heath hides this gem housed in a 19th-century cottage with a gorgeous beer garden. The interior is wonderfully cosy, with dark-wood tables, upholstered chairs and an assortment of distressed sofas. It serves Pimms and lemonade in summer and mulled wine in winter, both ideal after a long walk. The food (mains £14 to £16) is good too. (www.thegarden gatehampstead.co.uk)

Entertainment

Green Note LIVE MUSIC

13 ⭐ MAP P174, E4

Camden may be the home of punk, but it also has the Green Note: one of the best places in London to see live folk and world music, with gigs every night of the week. The setting is intimate: a tiny bare-brick room with mics set up in a corner, backdropped by red curtains. Online booking advised (tickets around £13). (www.greennote.co.uk)

KOKO LIVE MUSIC

14 ⭐ MAP P175, F5

Like a phoenix rising from the ashes, KOKO has emerged from its devastating 2020 fire as even better and more spectacular than before. Once the legendary Camden Palace, where Charlie Chaplin, the Goons and the Sex Pistols performed, and where Prince played surprise gigs, the theatre has a dance floor and decadent balconies, and now

North London Sounds 🎧

North London is the home of indie rock, and many a famous band started out playing in the area's grungy bars. Indeed, Camden High St has become a rock music Walk of Fame, with the unveiling of a granite plaque dedicated to the Who, the first of a planned 400. You can be sure to find live music of some kind every night of the week. A number of venues are multipurpose, with gigs in the first part of the evening (generally around 7pm or 8pm), followed by club nights beginning around midnight.

Charity Shop Treasures

Word on the street is that the nicer the neighbourhood, the better the charity shops. This clearly holds true for Primrose Hill, where three phenomenal charity shops crowd on Regents Park Road. Forget rummaging through bins and baskets: this is boutique territory, where racks have been carefully curated by colour-schemes and sizes, and everything is in immaculate condition. Grown-ups will love **Mary's Living & Giving Shop** (www.savethechildren. org.uk/shop/marys-living-and-giving-shops) and **Shelter** (www. shelter.org.uk/) for affordable fashion, including designer pieces at bargain prices, accessories and books. **FARA Kids** (www.fara charity.org/shop/primrose-hill) is a dream for parents and children alike: finally there's somewhere where you can let your children pick something they like or a new toy without having to worry about the price tag. All these shops are run by volunteers and proceeds help support the respective charities' work.

phenomenal acoustics as well. There are live bands most nights and hugely popular club nights on Saturdays. (www.koko.co.uk)

Jazz Cafe
LIVE MUSIC

15 ⭐ MAP P174, E4

The name would have you think jazz is the main staple, but it's only a small slice of what's on offer here. The intimate club-like space also serves up funk, hip-hop, R&B, soul and rare groove, with big-name acts regularly playing daily at 7pm. Friday (world music) and Saturday (soul, disco and house) club nights start at 10.30pm. (www. thejazzcafelondon.com)

Cecil Sharp House
TRADITIONAL MUSIC

16 ⭐ MAP P174, D4

Home to the English Folk Dance and Song Society, this institute keeps all manner of folk traditions alive. Performances and classes range from traditional British music and ceilidh dances to bell-jingling Morris dancing and clog-stamping, all held in its mural-covered Kennedy Hall. The dance classes are oodles of fun and there's a real community vibe; no experience necessary. (www.efdss.org/cecil-sharp-house)

Walking Tour

Walking on Hampstead Heath

Sprawling Hampstead Heath, with its rolling woodlands and meadows, feels a million miles away from central London. Covering 320 hectares, it's home to about 180 bird species, a rich mix of flora and expansive views from the top of Parliament Hill. The heath is particularly busy with families and dog walkers at weekends, and picnicking friends on sunny days.

Getting There

Ⓤ Hampstead station on the Northern Line. For Highgate Cemetery, get off at Archway (Bank branch of the Northern Line).

🚆 Hampstead Heath and Gospel Oak on the Overground.

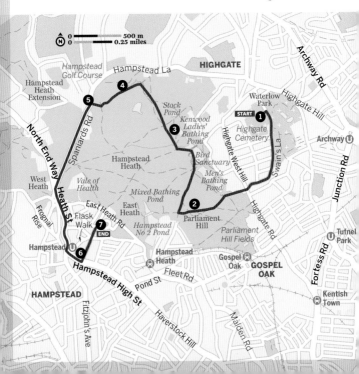

❶ Highgate Cemetery

Final resting place of Karl Marx, George Eliot (Mary Ann Evans) and Russian secret-service agent Alexander Litvinenko (who was poisoned with radioactive polonium-210 in 2006), Highgate Cemetery (www.highgatecemetery. org) is divided into East and West. To visit the atmospheric West Cemetery, you must take a tour.

❷ Parliament Hill

Head down Swain's Lane to Highgate West Hill roundabout and climb to **Parliament Hill** (p176) for all-inclusive views south over town. Spot the landmarks from the Shard to Parliament. Londoners and visitors love to picnic up here – choose your spot, tuck into some sandwiches and feast on the superb vistas.

❸ Hampstead Heath Ponds

You have a choice of three bathing ponds (men's, women's and a mixed pond) to take a dip at the Heath (BYO swimsuit and towel). The women's pond is the most tucked away and has a particularly bucolic feel. Both the men's and women's ponds are open year-round for cold-water swimming enthusiasts and are supervised by lifeguards. Prebooking a swim slot (go to www.cityoflondon.gov.uk) is necessary during peak times, like the middle of the day in summer.

❹ Kenwood House

Traverse the heath to the magnificent neoclassical 18th-century Kenwood House (www.english-heritage.org.uk/visit/places/kenwood) in a glorious sweep of perfectly landscaped gardens leading down to a picturesque pond. The house contains a magnificent collection of art, including paintings by Rembrandt, Constable, Turner, Gainsborough and Vermeer. Seek out the Henry Moore and Barbara Hepworth sculptures in the grounds.

❺ Spaniard's Inn

At the heath's edge is this marvellous 1585 tavern, where Romantic poets Keats and Byron and artist Sir Joshua Reynolds all paused for a tipple. The Spaniard's Inn (www.thespaniardshampstead.co.uk) has kept its historic charm – wood panelling, jumbled interior and hearty welcome – and is hugely popular with dog walkers, families and parkgoers on weekends.

❻ Explore Hampstead

Take bus 210 to Jack Straw's Castle stop and walk through this historic neighbourhood. Loved by artists in the interwar years, it has retained a bohemian feel, with sumptuous houses, leafy streets, cafes and lovely boutiques.

❼ Dinner at The Wells

Finish your afternoon on the Heath with a meal at the back-street gastropub, the Wells Tavern (www.thewellshampstead.co.uk), where you'll be rewarded with innovative takes on British fare in its gorgeous upstairs dining rooms.

Explore ⊛
Shoreditch
& the East End

These historic neighbourhoods contain some significant sights (mainly around Clerkenwell and Spitalfields) but are better known for culture, street art and nightlife. Shoreditch and Hoxton are the places for music, dancing and drinking with a mix of pubs, bars and small clubs. These are some of London's most colourful neighbourhoods, punctuated by excellent restaurants and vintage clothes stores.

The Short List

○ **Shoreditch nightlife (p191)** *Donning your hippest outfit and heading to Shoreditch for cocktails.*

○ **Super Market Sunday (p187)** *Crawling the markets with the multicultural masses along Columbia Rd and Brick Lane.*

○ **Old Spitalfields Market (p192)** *Searching out treasure and stopping for a bite to eat.*

○ **Dennis Severs' House (p189)** *Entering the quirky time capsule that is this 18th-century Huguenot abode.*

○ **Brawn (p190)** *Soaking up local East London life at this Mediterranean-inspired neighbourhood restaurant.*

Getting There & Around

Ⓤ Liverpool St is the closest stop to Spitalfields. Old St is the best stop for the western edge of Hoxton and Shoreditch.

🚇 Shoreditch High St and Hoxton are the closest overground stations to Spitalfields and the eastern parts of Shoreditch and Hoxton.

🚌 Useful buses include the 8, 55 and 242.

Shoreditch & the East End Map on p188

Columbia Road Flower Market (p187) MIKECPHOTO/SHUTTERSTOCK ©

Walking Tour

A Sunday in the East End

The East End has a colourful and multicultural history. Waves of migrants (French Protestant, Jewish, Bangladeshi) have left their mark on the area, which, added to the Cockney heritage and the 21st-century hipster phenomenon, has created an incredibly vibrant neighbourhood. It's best appreciated on Sundays, when the area's markets are in full swing.

Walk Facts

Start Columbia Road Flower Market; Ⓤ Hoxton

End Spitalfields Market; Ⓤ Liverpool St

Length 1.4km, three to four hours

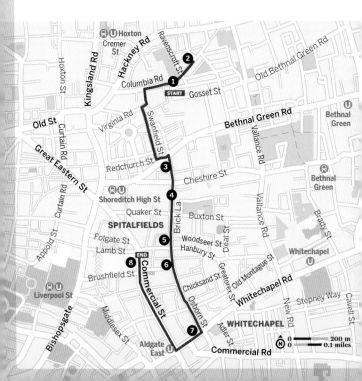

❶ Columbia Road Flower Market

This weekly market (www.columbiaroad.info) sells an amazing array of flowers and plants. It's lots of fun and the best place to hear proper Cockney barrow-boy banter. It gets packed, so go early.

❷ Royal Oak

Escape the crush in the wood-lined confines of the Royal Oak (www.royaloaklondon.com), a lovely old East End pub with a little garden out the back.

❸ Beigel Bake

Brick Lane was once the centre of the Jewish East End. Much of the Jewish community has moved to other areas but the no-frills Beigel Bake still does a roaring trade in dirt-cheap homemade bagels.

❹ Brick Lane Market

This street is best known for its huge Sunday market. You'll find anything from vintage to bric-a-brac, cheap fashion and food stalls.

❺ Old Truman Brewery

Founded in the 17th century and the largest brewery in the world by the 1850s, Truman's buildings and yards straddle both sides of Brick Lane. The complex now hosts edgy markets, including the funky **Sunday Upmarket** (www.sundayupmarket.co.uk), featuring young fashion designers.

❻ Brick Lane Great Mosque

No building better symbolises the waves of immigration in this area: the 1743 Huguenot New French Church was converted to a Methodist chapel in 1819, transformed into the Great Synagogue for Jewish refugees in 1898, before becoming the Great Mosque in 1976.

❼ Whitechapel Gallery

This ground-breaking gallery (www.whitechapelgallery.org) has no permanent collection, but hosts contemporary art exhibitions. It made its name by staging exhibitions by both established and emerging artists, including the first UK shows by Pablo Picasso and Frida Khalo.

❽ Old Spitalfields Market

Finish your walk at this former Victorian market space (p192) that's now home to small makers, vintage traders and independent retailers, plus a host of food vendors.

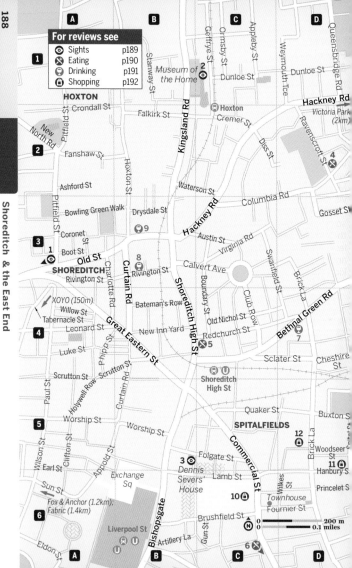

For reviews see
- ⊙ Sights   p189
- ✕ Eating   p190
- 🍷 Drinking   p191
- 🛍 Shopping   p192

A **B** **C** **D**

1
HOXTON
Crondall St
Falkirk St
Stanway St
Geffrye St
Ormsby St
Appleby St
Weymouth Tce
Dunloe St
Queensbridge Rd
Dunloe St

Museum of the Home 2 ⊙

2
New North Rd
Pitfield St
Fanshaw St
Hoxton St
Kingsland Rd
Hoxton ⊙
Cremer St
Diss St
Ravenscroct St
Hackney Rd
Victoria Park (2km)

3
Ashford St
Bowling Green Walk
Drysdale St
Waterson St
Columbia Rd
Gosset S
Coronet
🍷 9
1 ⊙
Old St
SHOREDITCH
Boot St
Rivington St
Charlotte Rd
Curtain Rd
8 ⊙
Rivington St
Hackney Rd
Austin St
Virginia Rd
Swanfield St
Brick La
Calvert Ave
Boundary St
Old Nichol St
Club Row
Shoreditch High St
Bethnal Green Rd
7 🛍

4
XOYO (150m)
Willow St
Tabernacle St
Leonard St
Pitfield St
Great Eastern St
Phipp St
Curtain Rd
New Inn Yard
Bateman's Row
✕ 5
Redchurch St
Sclater St
Cheshire St

5
Luke St
Scrutton St
Paul St
Holywell Row
Scrutton St
Worship St
Worship St
Shoreditch High St 🚇Ⓤ
Quaker St
Buxton S
SPITALFIELDS
12 🛍
Woodseer St
11 🛍
Hanbury S

6
Wilson St
Earl St
Clifton St
Appold St
Sun St
Exchange Sq
Bishopsgate
Fox & Anchor (1.2km); Fabric (1.4km)
Liverpool St 🚇Ⓤ
Ⓤ
Artillery La
Commercial St
Folgate St
3 ⊙
Dennis Severs' House
Lamb St
10 🛍
Brushfield St
Gun St
Townhouse
Fournier St
Wilkes St
Princelet S
6 ✕
Ⓝ
0   200 m
0   0.1 miles

Eldon St

Sights

Postal Museum & Mail Rail

MUSEUM

1 ◉ MAP P188, A3

Built in 1927 to beat traffic congestion, the Post Office Railway was
a subterranean train line used to
move four million pieces of mail
beneath the city streets every day
until it was shuttered in 2003. Revamped and opened to the public,
Mail Rail now delivers delighted
visitors around the once little-
known tracks below the largest
sorting office, in trains based on
the original designs. Follow it with
lessons on London's postcodes
and fun interactive displays for the
kids. (www.postalmuseum.org)

Museum of the Home

MUSEUM

2 ◉ MAP P188, B1

These beautiful ivy-clad brick
almshouses were built in 1714 as a
home for poor pensioners. Rooms
have since been furnished to
show how London residents lived
across the last 400 years. The
attention to detail is impressive,
down to the vintage newspaper
left open on the breakfast table.
(www.museumofthehome.org.uk)

Dennis Severs' House

HISTORIC BUILDING

3 ◉ MAP P188, B5

This extraordinary Georgian house
is set up as if its occupants – a

Postal Museum & Mail Rail

Tour Guide's Top Tips

Townhouse (www.townhous espitalfields.com) A bona-fide hidden gem in Spital-fields, this basement cafe, below an antique shop and gallery, is within a hugely atmospheric 1720s house. Find it at 5 Fournier Street.

Museum of London Dock-lands Step inside the former warehouses (www. museumoflondon.org.uk/docklands) of West India Dock to explore how the docks and the river made London the wealthiest city in the world during the 19th century. This free museum also has an excellent exhibition about the transatlantic slave trade and London's role in it.

Victoria Park Known as the People's Park (www. towerham lets.gov.uk/victoriapark), this 200+ acre public park opened in 1845 to give impoverished and overcrowded East Londoners a place to relax and have fun. Highlights include the canal towpath, Chinese Pagoda and two arches from the Old London Bridge.

Katie Wignall is a London Tour Guide and History blogger - @ look_uplondon

family of Huguenot silk weavers – have just walked out the door. Each of the 10 rooms is stuffed with the minutiae of everyday life from centuries past: half-drunk cups of tea, emptied but gleaming wet oyster shells and, in perhaps unnecessary attention to detail, a used chamber pot by the bed. It's more an immersive experience than a traditional museum; explorations of the house are conducted in silence. (www.dennissevershouse. co.uk)

Eating

Brawn   EUROPEAN ££

4 🍴 MAP P188, D2

There's a French feel to this relaxed corner bistro, yet the menu wanders into Italian and Spanish territory as well. Dishes are seasonally driven and delicious, and there's an interesting selection of European wine on offer. Booking ahead is recommended. (www.brawn.co)

Smoking Goat   THAI ££

5 🍴 MAP P188, C4

Trotting in on one of London's fleeting flavours of the week, Smoking Goat's modern Thai menu is top-notch. The industrial-chic look of exposed brick, huge factory windows and original parquet floors surround the open kitchen. It's a tough place for the spice-shy; cool down with a cold one from the exquisite cocktail list. (www.smokinggoatbar.com)

Victoria Park

Yuu Kitchen

ASIAN ££

6  MAP P188, C6

Manga images pout on the walls and birdcages dangle from the ceiling at this fun, relaxed place. Dishes are either bite-sized or designed to be shared, and while the focus is mainly Asian, some dishes from further along the Pacific Rim pop up too. Hence Filipino *lechon kawali* (slow-braised pork belly) sits alongside Vietnamese rolls and show-stopping *bao* (steamed buns). (www.yuukitchen.com)

Drinking

Cocktail Trading Co

COCKTAIL BAR

7 MAP P188, D4

In an area famous for its edgy, don't-give-a-damn attitude, this exquisite cocktail bar stands out for its classiness and cocktail confidence. The drinks (£11) are truly unrivalled, from flavours to presentation – bottles presented in envelopes, ice cubes as big as Rubik's Cubes and so on. The decor is reminiscent of a colonial-era gentlemen's club, just warmer and more welcoming. (www.thecocktailtradingco.com)

Callooh Callay
COCKTAIL BAR

8 🚇 MAP P188, B3

Given it's inspired by *Jabberwocky*, Lewis Carroll's nonsensical poem, this bar's eccentric decor is to be expected, and the top-notch cocktails have placed it on the 'World's 50 Best Bars' list multiple times. *Through the Looking Glass* isn't just the name of Carroll's novel here; try it yourself and see what happens. (www.calloohcallaybar.com)

Upper 5th Shoreditch
ROOFTOP BAR

9 🚇 MAP P188, B3

Set atop the Grade II–listed Courthouse Hotel in the centre of Shoreditch, this rooftop bar has fantastic views of London's skyline.During the week it's a great spot for a date – the atmosphere is lively but tables are spaced far enough apart to ensure privacy. On weekends it's more of a party venue. Prebook a table (minimum spend required) or chance it at the door. (www.shoreditch.courthouse-hotel.com)

Shopping

Old Spitalfields Market
MARKET

10 🔒 MAP P188, C6

Traders have been hawking their wares here since 1638, and it's still one of London's best markets. Sundays are the biggest days, but Thursdays are good for antiques, and crates of vinyl take over every other Friday. The market has upped its foodie credentials with multiple food counters that are the perfect antidote to the mostly bland chain restaurants on the market's periphery. (www.oldspitalfieldsmarket.com)

Libreria
BOOKS

11 🔒 MAP P188, D5

Mismatched vintage reading lamps spotlight the floor-to-ceiling canary-yellow shelves at this delightful indie bookshop, where titles are arranged according to themes like 'wanderlust', 'enchantment for the disenchanted' and 'mothers, madonnas and whores'. Cleverly placed mirrors

---

Drinking Directions ⓘ

Shoreditch is the torch bearer of London's nightlife: there are dozens of bars, clubs and pubs, open virtually every night of the week (and until the small hours at weekends) and it can get pretty rowdy. Clerkenwell is more grown-up, featuring lovely historic pubs and fine cocktail bars. Spitalfields sits somewhere in between the two extremes and tends to be defined by its City clientele on weeknights and market-goers on Saturday and Sunday.

Georgian Spitalfields

Crowded around its famous market and grand parish church, Spitalfields has long been one of the capital's most multicultural areas. Waves of Huguenot (French Protestant), Jewish, Irish and, more recently, Indian and Bangladeshi immigrants have made Spitalfields home. To get a sense of what Georgian Spitalfields was like, branch off to Princelet, Fournier, Elder and Wilkes streets. Having fled persecution in France, the Huguenots set up shop here from the late 17th century, practising their trade of silk weaving.

add to the labyrinthine wonder of the space, which is punctuated with mid-century furniture that invites repose and quiet contemplation. (https://libreria.io)

Rough Trade East MUSIC

12 🔒 MAP P188, D5

It's no longer directly associated with the legendary record label (home to the Smiths, the Libertines and the Strokes, among others), but this huge record shop is still tops for picking up indie, soul, electronica and alternative music. In addition to an impressive selection of CDs and vinyl, it also dispenses coffee and stages gigs and artist signings. (www.roughtrade.com)

Worth a Trip 👀
See Stars at the Royal Observatory & Greenwich Park

◎ MAP P198

The Royal Observatory is where studies of the sea, stars and time converge. The prime meridian charts its line through the grounds of the observatory to divide the globe into the eastern and western hemispheres. The complex sits atop a hill within leafy and regal Greenwich Park, with iconic views of the River Thames and the skyscrapers of Canary Wharf.

www.rmg.co.uk/royal-observatory

Greenwich Park, Black-heath Ave

adult/child £16/8

⊗ 10am-5pm Sep-Jun, to 6pm Jul & Aug

Ⓤ Greenwich or Cutty Sar

Flamsteed House

Charles II ordered the construction of Christopher Wren–designed Flamsteed House, the original observatory building, on the foundations of Greenwich Castle in 1675 after closing the observatory at the Tower of London, allegedly because the ravens were pooing on the equipment. Today it contains the magnificent **Octagon Room** and the rather simple apartment where the Royal Astronomers and their families lived.

On the lower levels, you'll find the **Time Galleries**, which explain how the longitude problem – how to accurately determine a ship's east–west location – was solved through astronomical means and the invention of the marine chronometer.

Meridian Courtyard

In the Meridian Courtyard, where the globe is decisively sliced into east and west, visitors can delightfully straddle both hemispheres, with one foot on either side of the meridian line. Every day, the red **Time Ball** atop the Royal Observatory drops at 1pm, as it has done since 1833.

The Greenwich meridian was selected as the global prime meridian at the International Meridian Conference in Washington, DC, in 1884. Greenwich became the world's ground zero for longitude and standard for time calculations, replacing the multiple meridians that had existed before.

Greenwich was assisted in its bid by the earlier US adoption of Greenwich Mean Time or its own national time zones, though the majority of world trade already used sea charts that identified Greenwich as the prime meridian.

★ **Top Tips**

o Leave time to continue on to the wonderful Rose Garden in the spring; in winter head to Ranger's House to view the Wernher Art Collection (bookings with English Heritage).

o Pre-booking a combination Royal Museums Greenwich Day Pass gives you access to the Royal Observatory and Cutty Sark with a 25% saving.

✕ **Take a Break**

The Astronomy Centre has a cafe, or pack a picnic to devour in Greenwich Park. Down the hill, you can snack your way around Greenwich Market (p199).

★ **Getting There**

Ⓤ Take the DLR to Cutty Sark or Greenwich stations.

⚓ Boats run from several central London piers.

🚶 One of London's two under-river, pedestrian-only tunnels links Greenwich to the Isle of Dogs.

Camera Obscura

In a small brick structure next to the Meridian Courtyard, the camera obscura projects a live image of Queen's House (p199) – as well as the people moving around it and the boats on the Thames behind – on to a table.

Enter through the thick, light-dimming curtains and close them behind you to keep the room as dark as possible.

Astronomy Centre

The southern half of the observatory contains the informative (and free) **Weller Astronomy Galleries**, where you can touch an object as ancient as the sun: part of the Gibeon meteorite, a mere 4.5 billion years old.

Other exhibits include a 1780 orrery (mechanical model of the solar system, minus the as-yet-undiscovered Uranus and Neptune), astro documentaries and the opportunity to view the Milky Way in multiple wavelengths.

Peter Harrison Planetarium

The state-of-the-art **Peter Harrison Planetarium** (www.rmg.co.uk/whats-on/planetarium-shows) – London's only planetarium – can lay out the heavens on the inside of its roof. It runs several informative shows a day, including a programme for kids, and it's best to book in advance.

Peter Harrison Planetarium

Prime Target

On 15 February 1894, the Royal Observatory was the unexpected target of a bomb plot. The bomber – a 26-year-old French anarchist called Martial Bourdin – managed to blow his left hand off in the bungled attack and died from his wounds soon afterwards. The choice of the Royal Observatory as a target was never understood, but it was undamaged. The bombing later found literary recognition in Joseph Conrad's novel *The Secret Agent* and the anarchist appears in the TS Eliot poem *Animula* under the name Boudin.

Greenwich Park

Greenwich Park (www.royal parks.org.uk/parks/green wich-park) is one of London's loveliest expanses of green, with cherry blossoms, a **rose garden**, picturesque walking paths, a 5th-century Anglo-Saxon **burial ground** and views of the financial district across the Thames from the crown of the hill.

Covering 74 hectares, it's the oldest enclosed royal park and is partly the work of André Le Nôtre, the landscape architect who designed the palace gardens of Versailles.

If you don't want to pay to enter the Meridian Courtyard, look out for the continuation of the prime meridian line, marked in metal, just outside the fence, where you can stand in two hemi-spheres at once for free.

Walking Tour 🥾

A Wander Around Historic Greenwich

If Greenwich's grand sights belonged to a British town beyond the capital, they would elevate it to one of the top destinations in the UK. That they belong to a district of London alone naturally makes this quaint Unesco-listed area a must-see neighbourhood. Fortunately, all of Greenwich's big-hitting sights are within an easily walkable area.

Getting There

Ⓤ Take the DLR to Cutty Sark or Greenwich stations.

⚓ Thames Clippers boats run to Greenwich and Royal Arsenal Woolwich from several central London piers.

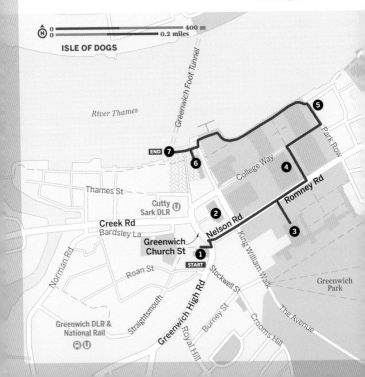

❶ St Alfege Church

Designed by Nicholas Hawksmoor to replace a 13th-century church, baroque St Alfege (www.st-alfege.org.uk) was consecrated in 1718 and features a restored mural by James Thornhill.

❷ Greenwich Market

Cross Greenwich Church St to Greenwich Market (www.greenwichmarket.london), one of London's smaller and more atmospheric covered markets, and snack your way through the 46 food stalls hawking homemade Jamaican rum cake, locally sourced oysters, Ethiopian vegetarian boxes, filled Brazilian churros and so much more.

❸ National Maritime Museum & Queen's House

Walk along Nelson Rd to the National Maritime Museum (www.rmg.co.uk/national-maritime-museum), which narrates the long, briny and eventful history of seafaring Britain. Continue the seafaring theme with a stop at nearby **Queen's House** (www.rmg.co.uk/queens-house), which has a gallery of portraits and other pieces with a maritime bent.

❹ Painted Hall

Cross Romney Rd to the grounds of the Old Royal Naval College, Greenwich's grandest collection of buildings. The recently restored Painted Hall (www.ornc.org), designed as a dining room for retired and disabled sailors and completed in 1726, is an over-the-top banqueting space covered floor-to-ceiling with the largest painting in Europe (children free).

❺ Trafalgar Tavern

Head to the Thames walkway and east to the elegant Trafalgar Tavern (www.trafalgartavern.co.uk), with crystal chandeliers, nautical decor and big windows overlooking the Thames.

❻ Cutty Sark

Follow the scenic path between the Thames and the Old Royal Naval College grounds to the Cutty Sark (www.rmg.co.uk/cuttysark), the last of the great clipper ships to sail between China and England in the 19th century.

❼ Greenwich Foot Tunnel

Descend the Greenwich Foot Tunnel and read its fascinating history, to cross under the Thames to the Isle of Dogs for expansive views of Greenwich from the north shore.

Worth a Trip 👀
Tour Regal Hampton Court Palace

London's most spectacular Tudor palace, 16th-century Hampton Court Palace is steeped in history, from the grand living quarters of Henry VIII to the spectacular gardens, complete with a 300-year-old maze. One of the best days out London has to offer, the palace is mandatory for anyone with an interest in British history, Tudor architecture or gorgeous landscaped gardens. Set aside plenty of time to do it justice.

www.hrp.org.uk/hampton courtpalace

Hampton Court Palace

adult/child £24.50/12.20

🕙10am-6pm, to 4.30pm Nov-Mar

🚢Hampton Court Palace

🚉Hampton Court

Entering the Palace

Passing through the magnificent main gate, you arrive first in the **Base Court** and beyond that **Clock Court**, named after its 16th-century astronomical clock. Off Base Court to the right as you enter is Andrea Magenta's nine-painting series **The Triumphs of Caesar** which portrays Julius Caesar returning to Rome in a triumphant procession. It was acquired by Charles I in 1629.

Henry VIII's State Apartments

The stairs inside Anne Boleyn's Gateway lead up to Henry VIII's Apartments, including the stunning **Great Hall**. The **Horn Room**, hung with impressive antlers, leads to the **Great Watching Chamber** where guards controlled access to the king.

Royal Pew & Henry VIII's Crown

Henry VIII's dazzling gemstone-encrusted crown has been re-created – the original was melted down by Oliver Cromwell – and sits in the Royal Pew, which overlooks the beautiful **Chapel Royal** (still a place of worship after 450 years).

Tudor Kitchens & Great Wine Cellar

Also dating from Henry's day are the delightful and phenomenally evocative Tudor kitchens, once used to rustle up meals for a royal household of some 1200 people. Don't miss the Great Wine Cellar, which handled the 300 barrels each of ale and wine consumed here annually in the mid-16th century.

★ **Top Tips**

o Check the website for activities and events.

o **Bushy Park** (www.royalparks.org.uk), a 445-hectare semi-wild expanse with herds of deer, is right next door.

✗ **Take a Break**

There are three cafes within the palace grounds: the **Tiltyard Cafe**, the **Privy Kitchen** and the **Fountain Court Cafe**. The gardens are huge, so pack a picnic if it's sunny.

★ **Getting There**

🚆 Hampton Court train station has services to/from London Waterloo.

⛴ Thames River Boats runs services here from Westminster (adult/child £22/12, three to four hours, April to September).

Cumberland Art Gallery

The restored Cumberland Suite off Clock Court is the venue for a staggering collection of artworks from the Royal Collection, including works by Rembrandt and Sir Anthony van Dyck's *Charles I on Horseback* (c 1635–36).

Cartoon Gallery

The Cartoon Gallery used to display the original Raphael Cartoons (now in the V&A Museum); nowadays it's just the late-17th-century copies.

William III's & Mary II's Apartments

A tour of William III's Apartments, completed by Wren in 1702, takes you up the grand **King's Staircase**. Highlights include the **King's Presence Chamber**, dominated by a throne backed with scarlet hangings. The sumptuous **King's Great Bedchamber**, with a bed topped with ostrich plumes, and the King's Closet (where His Majesty's toilet has a velvet seat) should not be missed.

The unique **Chocolate Kitchens** were built for William and Mary in about 1689. William's wife Mary II had her own apartments, accessible via the fabulous **Queen's Staircase** (decorated by William Kent).

Georgian Private Apartments

The Georgian Rooms were used by George II and Queen Caroline on the court's last visit to the palace in 1737. For a feel of life at court,

Sunken garden at Hampton Court Palace

Events & Activities

Check the schedule for details on spectacular shows and events, including Tudor jousting, falconry displays, ghost tours, garden adventures and family trails. In summer, fun 15- to 20-minute shire-horse-drawn **charabanc tours** (£10 per bench, which will seat up to the three people) depart from the East Front Garden between 11am and 5pm. **Luna Cinema** (www.thelunacinema.com) hosts outdoor films in summer at the palace. From November to mid-January you can glide (or slide) around the palace's glittering **ice rink**.

do sit down in the drawing room and have a go at one of the board games on display. Do not miss the fabulous Tudor **Wolsey Closet** with its early-16th-century ceiling and painted panels, commissioned by Henry VIII.

Gardens & Maze

Beyond the palace are the stunning gardens; keep an eye out for the **Real Tennis Court**, dating from the 1620s. Originally created for William and Mary, the **Kitchen Garden** is a magnificent re-creation.

No one should leave Hampton Court without losing themselves in the 800m-long **maze**, which is also accessible to those not entering the palace.

Survival Guide

Gherkin skyscraper (p124) ALEXANDER SPATARI/GETTY IMAGES ©
ARCHITECT: NORMAN FOSTER ©

Before You Go

Book Your Stay

○ Shoreditch, Kensington and South Bank are great places to stay.

○ London has some fantastic hotels, but demand often outstrips supply: book ahead, especially during summer and holidays.

○ Budgets under £100 per night get you a hostel bed (some are contemporary and stylish) or basic B&B. Look for online deals, business hotels in the City often have discounts for weekend stays.

○ B&Bs can have boutique-style charm, a lovely old building setting and a personal level of service.

○ For stays of a week or more, serviced apartments and short-term lets can be economical.

Useful Websites

○ **Visit London** (www. visitlondon.com) Huge range of listings; official tourism portal.

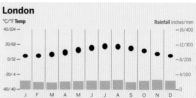

London

When to Go

○ **Winter (Dec–Feb)** Cold, short days with rain and occasional snow. Museums and attractions quieter.

○ **Spring (Mar–May)** Milder weather; trees in blossom, parks and gardens in bloom. Major sights begin to get busy.

○ **Summer (Jun–Aug)** Warm, sunny and light until late. High season. Expect crowds, but London's parks are lovely.

○ **Autumn (Sep–Nov)** Mild, sunny and colourful. Kids go back to school.

○ **London Town** (www. londontown.com) Last-minute offers on accommodation, restaurant and attractions.

○ **London Bed & Breakfast** (www.londonbb. com) B&B in private homes across the city.

○ **Lonely Planet** (lonelyplanet.com/england/london/hotels) Reviews and recommendations.

Best Budget

The Corner (www. thecornerlondoncity. co.uk) Well-designed little rooms available for a steal in East London.

Clink261 (www.clinkhostels.com/london/clink261) A big, well-run hostel near King's Cross.

Generator London (https://staygenerator.com/hostels/london) Large poshtel in leafy and central Bloomsbury.

St James Backpackers Hostel (www.saint-james-hostel.co.uk) Pocket-sized hostel in Earl's Court.

Best Midrange

CitizenM Tower of London (www.citizenm. com/destinations/

london/tower-of-london-hotel) Small but perfectly formed rooms, some with killer views.

Hoxton Southwark (https://thehoxton.com/london/southwark) Outstanding value, great location and gorgeous fit-out on the South Bank.

Hoxton Shoreditch (www.thehoxton.com/london/shoreditch/hotels) The hippest of hotels in the hippest London neighbourhood, Hoxton.

Best Top End

The Ned (www.thened.com) Heritage in the central financial district.

Number Sixteen (www.firmdalehotels.com/hotels/london/number-sixteen) Sophisticated and colourful with an idyllic garden in Kensington.

Hazlitt's (www.hazlittshotel.com) Old-world elegance in a terrific location in Soho.

Beaumont (www.thebeaumont.com) Art-Deco opulence and an excellent cocktail bar in Mayfair.

Arriving in London

Heathrow Airport

Some 15 miles west of central London, Heathrow Airport (LHR; www.heathrow.com) is one of the world's busiest, with four passenger terminals (numbered 2 to 5). It's Britain's main airport for international flights.

Underground Three Underground stations on the Piccadilly line serve Heathrow: one for Terminals 2 and 3, another for Terminal 4, and the terminus for Terminal 5. It's the cheapest way of getting to/from Heathrow; one-way paper tickets cost £6.30; Oyster or Contactless peak/off-peak costs £5.50/3.50. The journey to central London takes 45 minutes and trains depart every three to nine minutes. Services run from just after 5am to around midnight. The new Elizabeth Line serves all terminals. It is quicker than the Pic-

cadilly line (28 minutes to Paddington in central London) but more expensive (Oyster or Contactless peak/off-peak costs £12.80/10.80).

Train Heathrow Express (www.heathrow-express.com; one way/return £25/37, children free) links Heathrow with Paddington train station every 15 minutes. The journey takes just 15 minutes and trains run from around 5am to between 11pm and midnight.

Bus National Express (www.nationalexpress.com) coaches (one way from £6, 40 to 90 minutes, every 30 minutes to one hour) link Heathrow Central bus station with London Victoria coach station. The first bus leaves Heathrow Central bus station (at Terminals 2 and 3) around 4am, with the last departure around 1am. The first bus leaves Victoria at 2am, the last at around midnight. At night, the N9 bus (£1.65, 1½ hours, every 30 minutes) connects Heathrow Central bus station (and Heathrow Terminal 5) with central London, terminating at Aldwych.

Taxi A metered black-cab trip to/from central London will cost between £52 and £100 and take 45 minutes to an hour, depending on traffic.

Gatwick Airport

Located some 30 miles south of central London, Gatwick (LGW; www.gatwick-airport.com) is smaller than Heathrow and is Britain's number-two airport, mainly for international flights. The North and South Terminals are linked by a 24-hour shuttle train (three minutes).

Train National Rail (www.nationalrail. co.uk) has regular train services to/from London Bridge (30 to 45 minutes, every 15 to 30 minutes), London King's Cross (45 to 55 minutes, every 15 to 30 minutes) and London Victoria (30 minutes, every 10 to 15 minutes). Fares vary depending on the time of travel and the train company, but allow £12 to £20 for a single.

Gatwick Express

Trains (www.gatwickexpress.com; £20.60 one way without advanced booking) run every 15 minutes from the station near Gatwick South Terminal to London Victoria. From the airport, there are services between 5.45am and 11pm. From Victoria, they leave between 5.15am and 11pm. The journey takes 30 minutes.

Bus National Express (www.nationalexpress. com) coaches run throughout the day and night between Gatwick and London Victoria coach station (one way from £10). Journey time is between two and three hours, depending on traffic.

Taxi A metered black-cab to/from central London costs £100 to £120 and takes just over an hour. Uber and minicab companies are usually cheaper.

Stansted Airport

Stansted (STN; www. stanstedairport.com) is 35 miles northeast of central London in the direction of Cambridge. An international airport, Stansted serves a multitude of mainly European destinations and is served primarily by low-cost carriers such as Ryanair.

Train Stansted Express (www.stanstedexpress. com) (£20.70, service 45 minutes, every 30 minutes) links the airport and Liverpool St station. From the airport, trains leave from 5.30am to 12.30am. Trains depart Liverpool St station from 4.10am to 11.25pm.

Bus National Express (www.nationalexpress. com) coaches run around the clock, offering well over 100 services per day.

o Airbus A6 (from £15, one hour to 1½ hours) runs every 20 minutes to Victoria Coach Station via Marble Arch, Baker St and a couple more stops in north London.

o Airport A9 (from £15, one hour and 20 minutes) runs every 30 minutes to Stratford in east London.

Taxi A metered black cab trip to/from central London costs around £130 and takes at least an hour, depending on traffic and your destination. Uber and other minicabs are cheaper.

Luton Airport

A smallish, single-runway airport 32 miles northwest of London, Luton (LTN; www.london-luton.co.uk) generally caters for cheap charter flights and discount airlines.

Train National Rail (www.nationalrail.co.uk) has 24-hour services (£16.50, 40 minutes, every 10 minutes at peak times) from London St Pancras International to Luton Airport Parkway station, from where an airport shuttle bus (one way/return £2.40/3.80) will take you to the airport in 10 minutes.

Bus There are a couple of services that run around the clock between London Victoria Coach Station and Luton Airport. Airbus A1 (£12, 1¾ hours) runs over 60 times daily. Green Line Bus 757 (£11.50, 75 to 90 minutes) runs every 30 minutes.

Taxi A metered black cab trip to/from central London costs around £120 and takes at least an hour, depending on traffic. Uber and other minicabs are cheaper.

St Pancras International Station

Eurostar (www.eurostar.com) high-speed passenger rail service links London St Pancras International with Paris (2¼ hours), Brussels (1¾ hours), Amsterdam (3¾ hours) and other European cities. It has up to 15 daily departures. Fares vary greatly, from £39 one way standard class to more than £300 one way for a fully flexible business premier ticket. It pays to book well ahead and to be flexible with travel times for the cheapest fares.

Getting Around

Underground, DLR & Overground

○ Public transport in London is excellent, if pricey.

○ The **London Underground** ('the Tube'; 11 colour-coded lines) is part of a system that also includes **Docklands Light Railway** (DLR; www.tfl.gov.uk/dlr; a driverless overhead train operating in the eastern part of the city), the **Overground** network (mostly outside of Zone 1 and sometimes underground) and the new **Elizabeth line** (a new line running east–west across London).

○ It is overall the quickest and easiest way of getting around the city. It's always cheaper to travel with an Oyster Card or contactless payments (unless you're paying international transaction fees) than to buy a paper ticket. Children under 11 travel free.

○ First trains operate from around 5.30am Monday to Saturday and 6.45am Sunday. Last trains leave around 12.30am Monday to Saturday and 11.30pm Sunday.

○ Selected lines (the Victoria and Jubilee lines, plus most of the Piccadilly, Central and Northern lines) run all night on Friday and Saturday on what is called the 'Night Tube'.

○ London is divided into nine concentric fare zones.

Oyster Card

The Oyster Card is a smart card on which you can store credit towards 'prepay' fares, as well as Travelcards valid for periods from a day to a year. Oyster Cards are valid across the entire public transport network in London.

All you need to do when entering a station is touch your card on a reader (which has a yellow circle with the image of an Oyster Card on it) and then touch again on your way out. The system will then deduct the appropriate amount of credit from your card, as necessary. For bus journeys, you only need to touch once upon boarding. Note that some train stations don't have exit turnstiles, so you will need to tap out on the reader before leaving the station; if you forget, you will be hugely overcharged.

The benefit lies in the fact that fares for Oyster Card users are lower than standard ones. If you are making many journeys during the day, you will never pay more than the appropriate Travelcard (peak or off-peak) once the daily 'price cap' has been reached.

o Oyster Cards can be bought (£5 refundable deposit required) and topped up at any Underground station, travel information centre or shop displaying the Oyster logo. To get your deposit back along with any remaining credit, simply return your Oyster Card at a ticket booth.

o Contactless bank cards and Apple/Google Pay can now be used directly on Oyster Card readers and are subject to the same Oyster fares. The advantage is that you don't have to bother with buying, topping up and then returning an Oyster Card, but foreign visitors should bear in mind the cost of international transactions.

Bus

o Red double-decker buses afford great views of the city, but the going can be slow in heavy traffic.

o There are excellent bus maps at bus stops detailing routes and destinations serving the local area.

o The City Mapper app is also very helpful for trip planning and live updates on bus arrival times.

o Cash cannot be used on London's buses. Instead you must pay with an Oyster Card, Travelcard or a contactless payment card. Bus fares are a flat £1.65, no matter how fare you travel.

o Bus services normally operate from 5am to 11.30pm.

o More than 50 nightbus routes (prefixed with the letter 'N') run from around 11.30pm to 5am.

o Oxford Circus, Tottenham Court Rd and Trafalgar Sq are the main hubs for night routes.

o Children under 11 travel free; 11 to 15 year olds are half-price if registered on an accom-

Electric scooters

London is running an e-scooter hire scheme until May 2024 whereby you can rent an electric scooter in one location and then drop it off at another. There are three licensed providers – **Dott** (https://ridedott.com), **Lime** (www.li.me) and **TIER** (www.tier.app) – whose colourful electric scooters you will find across the city. Important things to note about the scheme:

o Speed is capped at 12.5mph. You'll go much faster on a bike.

o Download one of the providers' apps to register: you'll need an ID and driver's licence.

o Riders must be over the age of 18.

o E-scooters must be parked on designated bays and you must ride in cycle lanes; apps will show you where and point out any restrictions.

o Scooters cost £1 to unlock and £0.17 per minute thereafter.

panying adult's Oyster Card (register at a Zone 1 or Heathrow Tube station).

Bicycle

o Santander Cycles (www.tfl.gov.uk/modes/cycling/santander-cycles) are straightforward and particularly useful for visitors.

o Pick up a bike from one of the 800 docking stations dotted around the capital. Drop it off at another docking station.

o The access fee is £1.65 for 24 hours. Insert your debit or credit card in the docking station to pay your access fee.

o The first 30 minutes are free, then it's £1.65 for any additional period of 30 minutes (the pricing structure encourages short journeys).

o Take as many bikes as you like during your access period (24 hours), leaving five minutes between each trip.

o If the docking station is full, consult the terminal to find available docking points nearby.

Taxi

o Black cabs are available for hire when the yellow sign above the windscreen is lit; just stick your arm out to signal one.

o Fares are metered, with the flag fall charge of £3.80 (covering the first 248m during a weekday), rising by increments of 20p for each subsequent 124m.

o Fares are more expensive in the evenings and overnight.

o You can tip taxi drivers by 10%, but most Londoners simply round up to the nearest pound.

o Apps such as Gett (https://gett.com/uk/city/london) use your smartphone's GPS to locate the nearest black cab.

o Most Londoners tend to use Uber, which is cheaper than black cabs and can be booked.

o Minicabs, which are also licensed, offer similar prices to Uber.

They can't be hailed on the street and must be hired by phone, online or via an app.

• Minicabs don't have meters; there's usually a fare set by the dispatcher. Make sure you ask before setting off.

• Addison Lee (www. addisonlee.com) is a reputable minicab service.

• Apps such as Kabbee allow you to pre-book a minicab.

Boat

Uber Boat (www. thamesclippers.com) runs regular services between Embankment, Waterloo (London Eye), Blackfriars, Bankside (Shakespeare's Globe), London Bridge, Tower Bridge, Canary Wharf, Greenwich, North Greenwich and Woolwich piers (all zones adult/child £14.70/7.35), from 6.55am to around midnight (from 9.29am weekends). Use an Oyster card for slightly cheaper fares or check out the 'Roamer' ticket if you're doing more than one trip. You can also book directly through the Uber app.

Thames River Boats (www.wpsa.co.uk) run between April and September to Hampton Court Palace from Westminster Pier in central London (via Kew and Richmond). The sailing takes 3½ hours. Tickets from Westminster to Kew/Richmond/Hampton cost £16.50/18.50/22.

Car & Motorcycle

• Expensive parking charges, traffic jams, high petrol prices, efficient traffic wardens and wheel-clampers make driving unattractive for most Londoners.

• There is a congestion charge of £15 per day in central London. For full details check https://tfl. gov.uk/modes/driving/congestion-charge.

• It is illegal to use a mobile phone to call or text while driving (using a hands-free device to talk on your mobile is permitted).

• Cars drive on the left.

• All drivers and passengers must wear seat belts and motorcyclists must wear a helmet.

Essential Information

Accessible Travel

• For travellers with access needs, London is a frustrating mix of user-friendliness and head-in-the-sand disinterest. Visitors with vision, hearing or cognitive impairments will find their needs met in a piecemeal fashion.

• New hotels and modern tourist attractions are legally required to be accessible to people in wheelchairs, but many historic buildings, B&Bs and guesthouses are in older buildings, which are hard or prohibitively expensive to adapt.

• As a result of hosting the 2012 Olympics and Paralympics, and thanks to a forward-looking tourist board in VisitEngland, things are improving all the time.

• A third of Tube stations, half of overground stations, most piers, all tram stops, all Elizabeth line and DLR stations and the cable car have step-free access.

Dos & Don'ts

Although largely informal in their everyday dealings, Londoners do observe some (unspoken) rules of etiquette.

Strangers Unless asking for directions, British people generally won't start a conversation at bus stops or on Tube platforms. More latitude is given to non-British people.

Queues The British don't tolerate queue jumping. Any attempt to do so will receive tutting and protest.

Tube Stand on the right and pass on the left while riding an Underground escalator.

Bargaining Haggling over the price of goods (but not food) is OK in markets, but nonexistent in shops.

Punctuality It's not good form to turn up more than 10 minutes late for drinks or dinner. If you're unavoidably late, keep everyone in the loop.

Apologise The British love apologising. If you bump into someone on the Tube, say sorry; they may apologise back, even if it's your fault.

○ Buses can be lowered to street level when they stop and wheelchair users travel free.

○ All black cabs are wheelchair-accessible, but power wheelchair users should note that the space is tight and sometimes headroom is insufficient.

○ Guide dogs are welcome on public transport and in hotels, restaurants, attractions etc.

○ Download Lonely Planet's free AccessibleTravel guide from https://shop.lonely planet.com/categories/accessible-travel.com.

Business Hours

Banks 9am to 5pm Monday to Saturday

Post offices 9am to 5.30pm Monday to Friday and 9am to noon Saturday

Pubs & bars 11am to 11pm (many are open later)

Restaurants noon to 2.30pm and 6pm to 11pm

Sights 10am to 6pm

Shops 9am to 7pm Monday to Saturday, noon to 6pm Sunday

Discount Cards

London Pass (www. londonpass.com; 1/2/3/6/10 days £79/103/123/141/161) offers free entry and queue jumping at major attractions; check the website for details.

Electricity

Type G
230V/50Hz

Emergencies

Dial ☎999 to call the police, fire brigade or ambulance.

Money

o The unit of currency in the UK is the pound sterling (£).

o One pound sterling consists of 100 pence (called 'p' colloquially).

o Notes come in denominations of £5, £10, £20 and £50; coins are 1p, 2p, 5p, 10p, 20p, 50p, £1 and £2.

ATMs

o ATMs (cashpoints) generally accept Visa, Mastercard, Cirrus or Maestro cards. There is often a transaction surcharge for cash withdrawals with foreign cards.

o Non-bank-run ATMs that charge £1.50 to £2 per transaction are usually found inside shops. Look for 'Free cash' signs to avoid these.

Changing Money

o The best place to change money free from commission is in any local post-office branch.

o You can also change money in most high-street banks and some travel agencies, as well as at the numerous bureaux de change throughout the city.

Credit & Debit Cards

o Credit and debit cards are accepted almost universally.

o American Express and Diners Club are far less widely used than Visa and Mastercard.

o Contactless cards and smartphone payments are widespread. Transactions are limited to a maximum of £100.

Tipping

o Many restaurants add a 'discretionary' service charge to your bill.

o In places that don't automatically add this, you are expected to leave a 10% tip (unless service was unsatisfactory).

o There's no expectation to tip at the pub for drinks service.

Public Holidays

New Year's Day
1 January

Good Friday Late March/April

Easter Monday Late March/April

May Day Holiday First Monday in May

Spring Bank Holiday Last Monday in May

Summer Bank Holiday Last Monday in August

Christmas Day 25 December

Boxing Day 26 December

Safe Travel

o London's a fairly safe city considering its size, so exercising common sense should be enough to avoid any incidents.

o With COVID-19 rules in constant flux, carry a face mask in case you're requested to wear one.

Smoking

o Smoking is forbidden in all enclosed public places. Pubs sometimes have a designated smoking spot outside, often on the pavement.

o A lot of venues have no-vaping policies. Vaping is not allowed on public transport either.

Telephone

o The rare public phone (usually at train stations), should you need one, accepts coins or credit cards.

o British Telecom's famous red phone boxes survive in conservation areas only (notably Westminster).

Money-Saving Tips

o Visit free museums and sights.

o Buy an Oyster card.

o Take the bus, or even cheaper: walk!

o Carry a bottle with you: there are water fountains at most Tube stations and attractions.

o Bring your own travel mug: most coffee shops will knock 20p or 30p off the price of your hot drink.

Calling London

o London's area code is 020, followed by an eight-digit number beginning with 7 (central London), 8 (Greater London) or 3 (nongeographic). You only need to dial the 020 when you are calling London from elsewhere in the UK or if you're dialling from a mobile.

o To call London from abroad, dial your country's international access code, +44 (the UK's country code), +20 (dropping the initial 0 from the area code), followed by the eight-digit landline number.

International Calls & Rates

o International calling cards with stored value (usually £5, £10 or £20) and a PIN are available

to call abroad from landlines and public phones.

o Everyone else uses VOIP technology such as Skype, Whatsapp and FaceTime.

Mobile Phones

It's usually better to buy a local SIM card from any mobile-phone shop, though in order to do that your handset from home must be unlocked.

Tourist Information

Visit London (www.visitlondon.com) can help with everything from attractions and events to tours and accommodation. Some can book theatre tickets. Kiosks are dotted about the city and can provide maps and brochures.

Heathrow Airport Tourist Office (www.visitlondon.com/tag/tourist-information-centre) Information on transport, accommodation, tours and more. You can buy Oyster cards, Travelcards and bus passes here too.

Other Tourist Offices At King's Cross St Pancras Station, Piccadilly Circus Underground Station, Liverpool Street Station, Victoria Station and Greenwich.

Visas

o Immigration to the UK is becoming tougher, particularly for those seeking to work or study. Check www.gov.uk/check-uk-visa, or with your local British embassy, for the most up-to-date information.

Behind the Scenes

Send Us Your Feedback

We love to hear from travellers – your comments help make our books better. We read every word, and we guarantee that your feedback goes straight to the authors. Visit **lonelyplanet.com/contact** to submit your updates and suggestions. Note: We may edit, reproduce and incorporate your comments in Lonely Planet products such as guidebooks, websites and digital products, so let us know if you don't want your comments reproduced or your name acknowledged. For a copy of our privacy policy visit lonelyplanet.com/legal.

Our Readers

Many thanks to the travellers who used the last edition and wrote to us with helpful hints, useful advice and interesting anecdotes.

Emilie Thanks

Thank you to Conrad Heine for company and good suggestions, Evonne O'Rourke for good times, Angela Tinson at LP and my husband, Adolfo, for his wise words.

Tasmin Thanks

Thanks to my co-writer Emilie Filou for the advice; Angela Tinson and Monique Choy and the rest of the LP crew; Max for joining me on the dining front; and Simon for the research.

Acknowledgements

Cover photograph: Front: Tower Bridge & City Hall, nautiluz56/Getty Images ©, London City Hall by Foster + Partners ©
Back cover photograph: Red phone box and bus, Jakub Barzycki/-Shutterstock ©
Photographs pp44-45 (clockwise from left): Jeff Whyte/Shutterstock ©; mikecphoto/Shutterstock ©; cowardlion/Shutterstock ©; Anton_Ivanov/Shutterstock ©

This Book

This 8th edition of Lonely Planet's London guidebook was researched and written by Emilie Filou and Tasmin Waby. The previous two editions were also written by Emilie, Tasmin, Peter Dragicevich, Steve Fallon, Damian Harper, Lauren Keith and Masovaida Morgan. This guidebook was produced by the following:

Commissioning Editor
Angela Tinson

Senior Product Editor
Sandie Kestell

Product Editor
Sarah Farrell

Cartographer
Rachel Imeson

Book Designer
Fabrice Robin

Editor Monique Choy

Cover Researcher
Hannah Blackie

Thanks to Alex Conroy, Peter Cruttenden, David Espinosa, Brian Johnson, Jo Maddox, Ollie Olanipekun, Gabrielle Stefanos, Katie Wignall

Index

See also separate subindexes for:

⊗ **Eating p220**
◷ **Drinking p221**
✿ **Entertainment p221**
🔒 **Shopping p221**

Sights 000
Map Pages **000**